Congressional
Research
Service

Terrorism and Transnational Crime: Foreign Policy Issues for Congress

John Rollins
Specialist in Terrorism and National Security

Liana Sun Wyler
Analyst in International Crime and Narcotics

June 11, 2013

Congressional Research Service

7-5700

www.crs.gov

R41004

Summary

This report provides an overview of transnational security issues related to patterns of interaction among international terrorist and crime groups. In addition, the report discusses the U.S. government's perception of and response to the threat. It concludes with an analysis of foreign policy options.

In recent years, the U.S. government has asserted that terrorism, insurgency, and crime interact in varied and significant ways, to the detriment of U.S. national security interests. Although unclassified anecdotal evidence largely serves as the basis for the current understanding of criminal-terrorist connections, observers often focus on several common patterns.

- **Partnership Motivations and Disincentives:** Collaboration can serve as a force multiplier for both criminal and terrorist groups, as well as a strategic weakness. Conditions that may affect the likelihood of confluence include demand for special skills unavailable within an organization, greed, opportunity for and proclivity toward joint ventures, and changes in ideological motivations.

- **Appropriation of Tactics:** Although ideologies and motivations of an organization may remain consistent, criminals and terrorists have shared similar tactics to reach their separate operational objectives. Such tactics include acts of violence; involvement in criminal activity for profit; money laundering; undetected cross-border movements; illegal weapons acquisition; and exploitation of corrupt government officials.

- **Organizational Evolution and Variation:** A criminal group may transform over time to adopt political goals and ideological motivations. Conversely, terrorist groups may shift toward criminality. For some terrorist groups, criminal activity remains secondary to ideological ambitions. For others, profit-making may surpass political aspirations as the dominant operating rationale. Frequently cited terrorist organizations involved in criminal activity include Abu Sayyaf Group (ASG), Al Qaeda's affiliates, D-Company, Kurdistan Worker's Party (PKK), Revolutionary Armed Forces of Colombia (FARC), Haqqani Network, and Hezbollah.

To combat these apparent criminal-terrorist connections, Congress has maintained a role in formulating U.S. policy responses. Moreover, recent Administrations have issued several strategic documents to guide U.S. national security, counterterrorism, anti-crime, and intelligence activities. In July 2011, for example, the Obama Administration issued the *Strategy to Combat Transnational Organized Crime*, which emphasized, among other issues, the confluence of crime and terrorism as a major factor in threatening the U.S. global security interests.

While the U.S. government has maintained substantial long-standing efforts to combat terrorism and transnational crime separately, Congress has been challenged to evaluate whether the existing array of authorities, programs, and resources sufficiently responds to the combined crime-terrorism threat. Common foreign policy options have centered on diplomacy, foreign assistance, financial actions, intelligence, military action, and investigations. At issue for Congress is how to conceptualize this complex crime-terrorism phenomenon and oversee the implementation of cross-cutting activities that span geographic regions, functional disciplines, and a multitude of policy tools that are largely dependent on effective interagency coordination and international cooperation.

Contents

Tables

Appendixes

Contacts

Introduction

Transnational terrorists and criminals may collaborate, appropriate shared tactics, and otherwise benefit from interaction, resulting in bolstered capabilities, enhanced organizational infrastructure, improved access to resources, and expanded geographic reach. Historical examples also indicate that terrorist and transnational criminal groups may evolve, converge, transform, or otherwise alter their ideological motivations and organizational composition to appear similar. Although information on the extent and nature of criminal-terrorist relationships, including their impact on U.S. national security, remains anecdotal, many view the potential confluence of criminal and terrorist actors, skills, resources, and violent tactics as a cause for concern.[1] Such enhancements may in turn lengthen the duration of insurgencies, extend the longevity and capabilities of criminal and terrorist organizations, and undermine the ability of fragile governments to exert full control of their territory.

Some analysts have identified a series of potentially disturbing patterns that has hastened the expansion of relationships between terrorist and transnational crime groups. First, criminal syndicates appear to be growing in size, scope, and ambition. Globalization has extended their transnational reach, while major developments in technology, trade, and the financial industry have provided them with opportunities to exploit vulnerabilities in emerging criminal sectors, such as cybercrime. Many now maintain a transnational footprint and a flexible and networked membership roster that can adapt more readily to new market niches and establish more fluid alliances with external individuals and groups.

Second, the nature and activities of terrorist organizations appear to have also changed. Terrorist groups today, particularly those that most threaten U.S. global interests, appear to be motivated primarily by religious rather than nationalist and ethnic separatist imperatives that were common in the 1960s and 1970s. This shift has resulted in extremist movements that elicit sympathy well beyond a specific country or geographic region.[2] Further, terrorist groups appear to have become more resilient, due to a combination of continued state sponsorship or support, as well as entrepreneurial expansion into profitable criminal activities.

Combined, these trends may suggest an increase in geographic overlap where criminals and terrorists could operate and interact. These patterns may also suggest greater blurring of distinctions between one group and the other, the adoption of activities often attributed to the other, or the ad hoc evolution of a group's objectives based on the security challenges they encounter.[3] Key nodes, where interaction is most likely, include prisons; cyberspace, particularly online opportunities for social networking; and ungoverned or difficult-to-govern spaces, which

---

[1] This report is based on unclassified interviews and open sources. While the focus of this report is on threats to U.S. security interests manifested from terrorist organization-international organized crime syndicate partnering arrangements, it is important to note that the issue has garnered the attention of the wider international security community.

[2] See for example Bruce Hoffman, *Inside Terrorism* (New York: Columbia University Press, 2006).

[3] An action pursued with one set of motivations can evolve into a different scenario based on the challenges the terrorist or criminal actors encounter and the response of the host government and global security community. Some suggest that one example of such a transformation was the January 2013 attack on Algeria's In-Amenas oil facility, where a kidnapping for ransom plot transformed into a hostage situation involving violence-based terrorist tactics. Notably, the attack was reportedly masterminded by Moktar Belmoktar, an illicit actor with longstanding ties to both Islamist groups and organized crime.

include regions plagued by endemic corruption, conflict or post-conflict zones where legitimate governance has yet to take root, border regions, free trade zones, and urban mega cities where pockets of poverty, violence, criminality, and impunity from national law prevails. Overlap may also be facilitated by the involvement of negligent or hostile governments and kleptocratic or criminal states that may consider sponsorship or support of criminal or terrorist activity of strategic value.

Perceived Threat

The U.S. government has asserted that terrorism, insurgency, and crime interact in varied and significant ways, to the detriment of U.S. national security interests. In January 2012, the Director of National Intelligence (DNI) reported to Congress that transnational organized crime and its links to international terrorism was among the nation's most pressing national security concerns, specifically identifying the following areas of concern for crime-terrorism interaction:

- **Nuclear proliferation:** "We are aware of the potential for criminal service providers to play an important role in proliferating nuclear-applicable materials and facilitating terrorism."

- **Kidnapping for ransom:** "Kidnapping for ransom is increasing in many regions worldwide and generates new and deep income streams for transnational criminal networks ... and terrorist networks."

- **Human smuggling:** "Those who smuggle humans illegally have access to sophisticated, forged travel papers and the ability to constantly change their smuggling routes—routes that may span multiple continents before reaching their destinations. Smugglers undermine state sovereignty and sometimes facilitate the terrorist threat."

- **Illicit finance:** "Terrorists and insurgents will increasingly turn to crime and criminal networks for funding and logistics, in part because of U.S. and Western success in attacking other sources of funding. Criminal connections and activities of both Hizballah and AQIM [Al Qaeda in the Islamic Maghreb] illustrate this trend."[4]

DNI James R. Clapper's testimony to Congress in 2012 reiterated the findings of the U.S. intelligence community's 2010 review of threats posed by transnational organized crime. In that review, the first of its kind in 15 years, the intelligence community ultimately concluded that such illicit networks have "dramatically" increased in size, scope, and influence internationally. A public summary of the assessment identified a "threatening crime-terror nexus" as one of five key threats to U.S. national security:

> Terrorists and insurgents increasingly will turn to crime to generate funding and will acquire logistical support from criminals, in part because of successes by U.S. agencies and partner nations in attacking other sources of their funding. In some instances, terrorists and insurgents prefer to conduct criminal activities themselves; when they cannot do so, they turn to outside individuals and facilitators. Proceeds from the drug trade are critical to the

---

[4] Prepared testimony of Director of National Intelligence (DNI) James R. Clapper, in U.S. Congress, Senate Select Committee on Intelligence, *Current and Projected National Security Threats to the United States*, S.Hrg. 112-481, 112th Cong., 2nd sess., January 31, 2012 (Washington, D.C.: U.S. Government Printing Office, 2012).

continued funding of such terrorist groups as the Taliban and the Revolutionary Armed Forces of Colombia (FARC). Terrorist organizations such as al-Shabaab and drug trafficking organizations such as the cartels based in Mexico are turning to criminal activities such as kidnapping for ransom to generate funding to continue their operations. Some criminals could have the capability to provide weapons of mass destruction (WMD) material to other terrorist groups, such as Hizballah and al-Qaida in the Islamic Maghreb, though the strength of these drug links and support remain unclear. U.S. intelligence, law enforcement, and military services have reported that more than 40 foreign terrorist organizations have links to the drug trade. Some criminal organizations have adopted extreme and widespread violence in an overt effort to intimidate governments at various levels.[5]

DNI Clapper's testimony to Congress in 2013 additionally noted that the U.S. intelligence community is "monitoring the expanding scope and diversity of 'facilitation networks,' which include semi-legitimate travel experts, attorneys, and other types of professionals, as well as corrupt officials, who provide support services to criminal and terrorist groups."[6]

Other U.S. government documents characterize the confluence of transnational organized crime and international terrorism as a growing phenomenon. Whereas in previous decades criminal and terrorism links occasionally occurred, such connections appear to be taking place with greater frequency today and may be evolving into more of a matter of practice rather than convenience. According to the U.S. Department of Justice (DOJ), recent investigations suggest that international organized criminals are willing to provide logistical and other support to terrorists.[7] According to the U.S. Drug Enforcement Administration (DEA), 19 of 49 (39%) State Department-designated foreign terrorist organizations (FTOs) have "confirmed links to the drug trade" as of November 2011.[8] In 2003, DEA reported that 14 of 36 (39%) FTOs were involved "to some degree" in illicit narcotics activity.[9] For FY2010, DOJ reported that 29 of the top 63 international drug syndicates, identified as such on the consolidated priority organization target (CPOT) list, were associated with terrorists.[10]

The State Department's 2012 *Country Reports on Terrorism* describes more than 20 FTOs as having financially profited from criminal activity to sustain their terrorist operations (see the **Appendix**).[11] Such listed FTOs include Al Shabaab, Army of Islam (AOI), Al Qaeda in the Arabian Peninsula (AQAP), Al Qaeda in Iraq (AQI), Al Qaeda in the Islamic Maghreb (AQIM), Abu Sayyaf Group (ASG), United Self-Defense Forces of Colombia (AUC), Continuity Irish Republican Army (CIRA), Communist Party of the Philippines (CPP), Revolution People's

---

[5] U.S. National Intelligence Council (NIC), *The Threat to U.S. National Security Posed by Transnational Organized Crime*, 2011.

[6] Prepared testimony of DNI Clapper, in U.S. Congress, Senate Select Committee on Intelligence, *Worldwide Threat Assessment of the U.S. Intelligence Community*, 113th Cong., 1st sess., March 12, 2013.

[7] U.S. Department of Justice (DOJ), *Overview of the Law Enforcement Strategy to Combat International Organized Crime*, April 2008.

[8] Prepared testimony of U.S. Drug Enforcement Administration (DEA) Special Operations Division Special Agent in Charge Derek S. Maltz, in U.S. Congress, House Committee on Foreign Affairs, Subcommittee on Terrorism, Nonproliferation, and Trade, *Narcoterrorism and the Long Reach of U.S. Law Enforcement, Part II*, Serial No. 112-81, 112th Cong., 2nd sess., November 17, 2011 (Washington, D.C.: U.S. Government Printing Office, 2011).

[9] Prepared testimony of DEA Assistant Administrator for Intelligence Steven W. Casteel, in U.S. Congress, Senate Committee on the Judiciary, *Narco-Terrorism: International Drug Trafficking and Terrorism—A Dangerous Mix*, S.Hrg. 108-173, 108th Cong., 1st sess., May 20, 2003 (Washington: D.C.: U.S. Government Printing Office, 2003).

[10] Obama Administration, *National Strategy to Combat Transnational Organized Crime*, July 2011.

[11] U.S. Department of State, *Country Reports on Terrorism 2012*, May 2013.

Liberation Party (DHKP/C), National Liberation Army (ELN), Revolutionary Armed Forces of Colombia (FARC), Moroccan Islamic Combatant Group (GICM), Hamas, Hezbollah, Haqqani Network (HQN), Jemaah Ansharut Tauhid (JAT), Jemaah Islamiya (JI), Lashkar I Jhangvi (LJ), Liberation Tigers of Tamil Eelam (LTTE), Kurdistan Workers' Party (PKK), Shining Path (SL), and Tehrik-e Taliban Pakistan (TTP).

Such government studies reinforce assessments from the late 1990s that predicted an increase in crime-terrorism interactions. For example, in 1997, a U.S. Department of Defense (DOD) task force study on transnational threats concluded that terrorists groups, religious extremists, anti-government militias, narcotics traffickers, and global criminals were "increasingly linked in new and more cooperative ways."[12] In 2000, a U.S. interagency assessment of international crime threats further highlighted growing crime-terrorism interactions.[13] The assessment identified the end of the Cold War as a major contributor to this development. As certain insurgent and extremist groups were no longer able to rely on Soviet-affiliated state sponsors for aid, some increasingly turned to crime as an alternative source of funds.[14] The assessment also concluded that most crime-terrorism interactions were often fleeting, or based on symbiotic arrangements that were nevertheless strained and marked by suspicion. Some groups, however, viewed criminal activity as not only a lucrative source of funding, but also an effective means to advance their political or ideological objectives.[15] Other groups, meanwhile, underwent transformations in which their primary organization motivations would shift from political to (illicit) profit-driven.

U.S. Government Strategies

To combat this apparent criminal-terrorist connection, recent Administrations have issued several key strategic documents to guide U.S. government efforts and approach the issue from the perspectives of national security, counterterrorism, anti-crime, and intelligence. The Obama Administration's key strategic documents are described below in chronological order.

In August 2009, the Obama Administration issued its **National Intelligence Strategy**, which included as a primary mission the goal of penetrating and supporting "the disruption of terrorist organizations and the nexus between terrorism and criminal activities."[16]

In May 2010, the Obama Administration issued its **National Security Strategy**, a broad-ranging document that identified key priorities for the United States.[17] One such priority was to combat "transnational criminal threats and threats to governance"—including the "crime-terror nexus."

---

[12] U.S. Department of Defense (DOD), Office of the Undersecretary of Defense for Acquisition and Technology, Defense Science Board, *1997 Summer Study Task Force on DOD Responses to Transnational Threats*, Vol. 1, final report, October 1997.

[13] Clinton Administration, *International Crime Threat Assessment*, December 2000.

[14] See also Steven Hutchinson and Pat O'Malley, "A Crime-Terror Nexus? Thinking on Some of the Links Between Terrorism and Criminality," *Studies in Conflict & Terrorism*, Vol. 30, No. 12, December 2007, pp. 1095-1107; Angel Rabasa et al., "Chapter Seven: The Convergence of Terrorism, Insurgency, and Crime," in *Beyond al-Qaeda, Part 2: The Outer Rings of the Terrorist Universe*, RAND Corporation, 2006, pp. 101-160.

[15] The report states that some groups, particularly those that controlled territory, would encourage illicit activity in the region to "isolate" it from the national economy, to "deprive the government of the region's economic productivity," and to "increase the dependence of the local population on their control and authority."

[16] Obama Administration, *National Intelligence Strategy of the United States of America*, August 2009.

[17] Obama Administration, *National Security Strategy*, May 2010.

The 2010 National Security Strategy encouraged a "multidimensional strategy" that emphasized citizen security and harm reduction, disruption and dismantling of illicit networks, and bolstering the capacity of foreign governments to enforce the rule of law.

In April 2011, the U.S. Department of Defense (DOD) issued a **Counternarcotics and Global Threats Strategy**.[18] The strategy describes an international security environment characterized by a "confluence of dispersed and decentralized global networks of criminals and terrorists." It further states that such networks are "composed largely of individuals and groups that receive occasional support from corrupt government officials" and "are loosely organized and ever-evolving, pragmatically appearing and disappearing for political-criminal gain." The DOD strategy identifies three strategic goals:

- to disrupt and disable actors and activities related to trafficking, insurgency, corruption, threat finance, terrorism, drug precursor chemical distribution in Afghanistan and Pakistan;

- to sharply reduce illicit drug and drug precursor chemical distribution, as well as related transnational organized criminal threats in the Western Hemisphere, particularly Mexico, Central America, Colombia, and Peru;[19] and

- to mitigate the size, scope, and influence of targeted transnational criminal organizations and trafficking networks such that they pose only limited, isolated threats to U.S. national and international security.

In June 2011, the Obama Administration issued its **National Strategy for Counterterrorism**. Included among its eight "overarching goals" was the goal to "deprive terrorists of their enabling means"—terrorist financing and the facilitation of terrorist travel, materiel smuggling, and communications.[20] The Administration's National Strategy for Counterterrorism sought to achieve this goal by

- blocking the flow of financial resources to terrorist groups through sanctions, prosecutions, international cooperation, and diplomatic pressure (money laundering and kidnapping for ransom); and

- working with international partners to identify and prevent terrorist groups from moving its recruits, operatives, and supplies across borders (human and weapons smuggling).

In July 2011, the Obama Administration issued its **Strategy to Combat Transnational Organized Crime**.[21] Among its primary objectives was to "defeat transnational criminal networks that pose the greatest threat to national security by targeting their infrastructures, depriving them of their enabling means, and preventing the criminal facilitation of terrorist activities." Key actions described by the strategy to combat the crime-terrorism nexus included the following:

---

[18] U.S. Department of Defense, *Department of Defense Counternarcotics and Global Threats Strategy*, April 27, 2011.

[19] Order of countries and regions as stated in the original text.

[20] Obama Administration, *National Strategy for Counterterrorism*, June 2011.

[21] Obama Administration, *Strategy to Combat Transnational Organized Crime*, July 2011.

- Enhancing intelligence collection on transnational organized crime threats, particularly the potential role of criminal groups in facilitating WMD terrorism.

- Exposing vulnerabilities in the international financial system that could be exploited by "terrorist and other illicit financial networks" and applying financial tools and sanctions against such networks.

- Establishing a "whole-of-government plan" to combat kidnapping for ransom as a means to finance terrorists, among other "bad actors."

- Developing a "comprehensive approach" to dismantling drug trafficking organizations with connections to terrorist groups.

- Enhancing foreign capabilities through counterterrorism capacity building, foreign law enforcement cooperation, military cooperation, and the strengthening of justice and interior ministries.

Patterns in Crime-Terrorism Interaction

Limited unclassified anecdotal evidence largely serves as the basis for the current understanding of criminal-terrorist connections. In the absence of comprehensive data, it is difficult to assess whether such anecdotal cases are indicative of a widespread problem, a growing trend, or isolated observation.[22] What is clear from existing literature on the subject, however, is that crime-terrorism interactions can vary significantly and change over time. The following sections summarize several common patterns of crime-terrorism links, with specific examples drawn from a range of court cases, reports, and news articles.

Partnership Motivations and Disincentives

The underlying rationales for criminal and terrorist group partnerships as well as the conditions that may facilitate the evolution or transformation of a criminal or terrorist group into the other may vary. Collaboration can serve as a force multiplier for both criminal and terrorist groups, bolstering their capabilities, strengthening their infrastructure, and increasing their wealth. On the other hand, partnering could also have the potential of sowing seeds for distrust and competition among illicit actors—vulnerabilities that could be exploited by international security authorities.[23]

From the perspective of a terrorist organization, the primary motivation for partnering or adopting criminal tactics would be to sustain and grow the organization for purposes of pursuing or financing its ideological-based activities. Out of this sense of perceived need, the organization may turn to or rely more heavily on partnering with criminal syndicates for continued viability. Common disincentives for partnering would include increased attention from government authorities; fear of compromising internal security; ideological resistance to illicit endeavors; and the availability of sufficient alternative funding sources, such as state sponsors.

---

[22] See also John T. Picarelli, "Osama bin Corleone? Vito the Jackal? Framing Threat Convergence Through an Examination of Transnational Organized Crime and International Terrorism," *Terrorism and Political Violence*, Vol. 24, No. 2 (2012), pp. 180-198.

[23] Such considerations are predicated on the theory that the leaders of an organization think rationally about the near- and long-term considerations and consequences, unintended or otherwise, of partnering with an entity that has differing motivations and ideologies.

From the perspective of a criminal syndicate, motivations for cooperating with terrorist organizations would include the near singular purpose of increasing its financial stature. As with terrorist organizations, common disincentives from the perspective of criminal groups may involve increased and unwanted attention from authorities, risk of infiltration, and heightened vulnerability of organization leadership to capture. Criminal groups already in control of lucrative revenue streams may not find the potential for additional business with terrorist groups sufficient to outweigh the costs. Criminal groups may also opt to avoid collaboration with terrorist groups if such interactions would disrupt their relationships with corrupt government officials who are willing to facilitate criminal activities, but not terrorism-related ones.

Conditions that may affect the likelihood of confluence include a lack of in-house capabilities and demand for special skills to conduct particular operations. Some groups may be more hesitant to collaborate with outsiders, depending in part on the nature of the operational environment, the presence of competitors, and the opportunity for contact with and the strength of relations between terrorist and criminal elements. Other barriers to cooperation may include cultural, religious, or ideological differences across groups. On the other hand, motivations such as greed or necessity for organizational viability or expansion may induce some groups to welcome or seek out external partners.

Individual groups may also transition along an apparent crime-terrorism continuum. Over time, ideologically motivated groups that initially avoid involvement with criminal activities may become increasingly attracted by the lucrative nature of criminal activities.[24] In other instances, criminal groups may become radicalized and apply their criminal expertise to conduct operations that not only result in lucrative illicit profits but also further ideologically oriented goals. In other situations, individuals in a terrorist organization may not follow leadership directives to stay away from individuals in a criminal organization (or vice versa) and may unilaterally develop external relationships. Some analysts suggest that this phenomenon may occur with greater regularity due to the increasingly decentralized nature of terrorist groups and other possible factors.[25]

Appropriation of Tactics

Criminals and terrorists often share similar tactics to reach their operational goals.[26] These include acts of terrorism and political violence; involvement in criminal activity for profit; money laundering; undetected cross-border movements; illegal weapons acquisition; and government corruption. Changes in the selection of tactics may signify shifts in the strength and capacity of an organization or the ideological desires of the organization's leadership. A criminal group under pressure by authorities or rival criminal groups may react by organizing violent attacks to intimidate the public and deter the government from future pursuit. A terrorist group's loss of state sponsorship may prompt it to find illicit alternatives for funding and operational support. The following sections describe several methods and tactics common to both criminal and

---

[24] See, for example, Karen Ballentine and Jake Sherman, eds., *The Political Economy of Armed Conflict: Beyond Greed and Grievance* (Boulder, CO: Lynne Rienner Publishers, 2003); Paul Collier and Anke Hoeffler, "Greed and Grievance in Civil War," *Oxford Economic Papers*, Vol. 56, No. 4 (2004), pp. 563-595.

[25] Richard Barrett, *The Economic Crisis: Al-Qaeda's Response*, Washington Institute for Near East Policy, Policywatch no. 1485, March 9, 2009.

[26] It should be noted that the adoption of a tactic by either a criminal or terrorist group that is traditionally used by the other entity in and of itself does not change the ideology, motivation, and goals of the organization or how it might be designated and approached by international security actors.

---

terrorist groups, including (1) the use of violence for political effect, (2) crime-for-profit activities, and (3) illicit support activity.

Violence for Political Effect

Although more commonly associated with terrorist groups, criminal groups have also occasionally used violence as a tactic to change political and public perceptions. Common past examples have included the use of terrorist-style violence, intimidation, and hostage-taking tactics by the Brazilian prison gang and drug trafficking organization (DTO) Primeiro Comando da Capital (PCC) in 2006.[27] In response to counternarcotics pressure in the 1980s and 1990s, the Medellin cartel conducted a wave of violent attacks on Colombian government and civilian targets, including the explosion of a commercial airliner and a truck bomb. The Italian mafia targeted prominent landmarks, politicians, and government officials in response to law enforcement pressure in the 1990s.[28]

Drug trafficking-related violence in Mexico, which surged in recent years due to a combination of increased counternarcotics pressure by the government and DTO-on-DTO competition, has at times appeared similar to

> **Further CRS Reading**
>
> For more information on DTOs in Mexico, see CRS Report R41576, *Mexico's Drug Trafficking Organizations: Source and Scope of the Violence*, by June S. Beittel.

terrorist-style attacks, with comparable tactics of intimidation.[29] Mexican government officials, for example, have been targeted by traffickers, at times in reprisal for their role in cartel arrests. In May 2008, one of Mexico's highest-ranking law enforcement officials, Edgar Millan Gomez, was assassinated in Mexico City by DTO-affiliated gunmen.[30] In other cases, drug traffickers have deployed small improvised explosive devices (IEDs) against law enforcement officials suspected of working for rival gangs.

Observers continue to debate whether the use of political violence as a tactic by Mexican DTOs warrants describing such groups as terrorist organizations. Most observers recognize that few instances of Mexican DTO violence appear to be motivated by ideology or a desire to overthrow the Mexican government.[31] According to the State Department's 2012 Country Reports on Terrorism, there was "no evidence that these criminal organizations had political or ideological motivations, aside from seeking to maintain the impunity with which they conduct their criminal activities."[32] Some have suggested that one of these exceptions may have occurred in September 2008, when a deadly attack on Mexico's Independence Day involving throwing grenades into a crowd of revelers that had gathered for a firework display was suspected to have been organized

---

[27] See for example Luciana M. Fernández, "Organized Crime and Terrorism: From the Cells Towards Political Communication, A Case Study," *Terrorism and Political Violence*, Vol. 21, No. 4 (2009), pp. 595-616.

[28] See also Louise I. Shelley and Picarelli, "Methods Not Motives: Implications of the Convergence of International Organized Crime and Terrorism," *Police Practice and Research*, Vol. 3 No. 4 (2002), pp. 305-318.

[29] See for example Sylvia M. Longmire and John P. Longmire IV, "Redefining Terrorism: Why Mexican Drug Trafficking is More Than Just Organized Crime," *Journal of Strategic Security*, Vol. 1, No. 1 (2008), pp. 35-51.

[30] James C. McKinley, "Gunmen Kill Chief of Mexico's Police," *The New York Times*, May 9, 2008; McKinley, "6 Charged in Shooting of Officer in Mexico," *The New York Times*, May 13, 2008.

[31] "Mexico: Rebranding the Cartel Wars," *Stratfor*, December 25, 2010; Scott Stewart, "The Perceived Car Bomb Threat in Mexico," *Stratfor*, April 13, 2011.

[32] U.S. Department of State, *Country Reports on Terrorism 2012*, May 2013.

by drug traffickers.[33] Yet, in this case, some traffickers appeared to distance themselves from the attack, joining in the victims' outcry and refusing to take responsibility for the attack. Other incidents that have raised questions about Mexican drug traffickers' motives and tactics include a casino fire that killed 52 civilians in 2011, and was allegedly instigated by Los Zetas.[34]

The Suspected 2011 Iranian Plot to Assassinate the Saudi Ambassador to the United States

Highlighting the potential for cooperation among organized crime and terrorist groups to plan and conduct an act of violence is the alleged plot to assassinate Saudi ambassador to the United States Adel al-Jubeir, publicly disclosed in October 2011.[35] According to U.S. authorities, Manssor Arbabsiar, a dual U.S.-Iranian national from Corpus Christi, TX, and several members of the Iran-based Islamic Revolutionary Guards Corps-Quds Force (IRGC-QF) planned to assassinate al-Jubeir by bombing a local restaurant he frequented and also by bombing the Saudi Arabian and Israeli embassies in Washington, DC.

As part of the alleged bombing plot, Arbabsiar arranged to hire members of the Mexican DTO Los Zetas to conduct the assassination for a fee of $1.5 million. A side deal was reportedly discussed in which several tons of opium from the Middle East would be trafficked to Mexico. The alleged plot, however, was discovered because Arbabsiar's Mexican DTO intermediary was in fact an informant for the DEA. Arbabsiar was ultimately arrested in New York and reportedly confessed to having been recruited, funded, and directed by the IRGC-QF to find Mexican DTO members to conduct the assassination plot. In conjunction with Arbabsiar's arrest, the U.S. Department of the Treasury announced financial sanctions against Arbabsiar and four others connected to the plot who were alleged members of the IRGC-QF, an organization that the Treasury Department had designated pursuant to Executive Order (EO) 13224 in October 2007. On October 17, 2012, Arbabsiar pleaded guilty in U.S. federal court to charges associated with the murder-for-hire plot.[36] In announcing the guilty plea, DEA Administrator Leonhart noted, "The dangerous connection between drug trafficking and terrorism cannot be overstated."[37] On May 30, 2013, Arbabsiar was sentenced to 25 years in prison.

Many observers have commented with incredulity that the IRGC-QF would partner with a non-Muslim DTO or use non-professional Iranian-American operatives such as Arbabsiar, and that senior Iranian authorities would authorize such an action on U.S. soil. It remains to be seen whether this alleged plot is indicative of greater crime-terrorism cooperation or a one-time departure from conventional IRGC-QF tactics. Other alleged plots, many of which appear to have also failed spectacularly, have been attributed in media reports to other Iranian sponsored groups, including Hezbollah.[38]

---

[33] "Mexico Independence Day Grenade Attack Kills 7," *USA Today*, September 16, 2008; Marc Lacey, "Grenade Attack in Mexico Breaks from Deadly Script," *The New York Times*, September 25, 2008; E. Eduardo Castillo, "Mexico Arrests 3 Suspects in Grenade Attack," *Associated Press*, September 27, 2008.

[34] Another exception may include the activities of the Mexican DTO La Familia Michoacana and its spin-off group Los Caballeros Templarios. Unlike other Mexican DTOs, this group purports to be motivated by both criminal and ideological rationales, describing itself as a religious organization and defender of local political grievances. Shawn Teresa Flanigan, "Terrorists Next Door? A Comparison of Mexican Drug Cartels and Middle Eastern Terrorist Organizations," *Terrorism and Political Violence*, Vol. 24, No. 2 (2012), pp. 279-294; Phil Williams, "The Terrorism Debate Over Mexican Drug Trafficking Violence," *Terrorism and Political Violence*, Vol. 24, No. 2 (2012), pp. 259-278.

[35] DOJ, "Two Men Charged in Alleged Plot to Assassinate Saudi Arabian Ambassador to the United States," press release, October 11, 2011; U.S. District Court, Southern District of New York (SDNY), *United States of America v Manssor Arbabsiar and Gholam Shakuri*, criminal complaint, October 11, 2011; U.S. Department of the Treasury, "Treasury Sanctions Five Individuals Tied to Iranian Plot to Assassinate the Saudi Arabian Ambassador to the United States," press release, October 11, 2011; Benjamin Weiser, "Not-Guilty Plea in Plot to Kill Saudi Ambassador to the U.S," *The New York Times*, October 24, 2011.

[36] DOJ, "Man Pleads Guilty in New York to Conspiring with Iranian Military Officials to Assassinate Saudi Arabian Ambassador to the United States," press release, October 17, 2012.

[37] Ibid.

[38] Nicholas Kulish, Eric Schmitt, and Matthew Brunwasser, "Bulgaria Implicates Hezbollah in July Attack on Israelis," *The New York Times*, February 5, 2013.

Crime-for-Profit

In addition to organized crime groups, some terrorist organizations may seek funding through criminal activities. Often, the potential profits associated with criminal activity are a motivating factor for both organized crime and terrorist groups. Since the end of the Cold War and corresponding declines in traditional state-sponsored sources of funding, some observers suggest that terrorist groups have become increasingly motivated to generate funds through criminal activity to sustain organizational capabilities. Heightened international counterterrorism measures in the past decade may have further depleted other traditional sources of funds, including private sector donations, which reinforce the desire for terrorist groups to seek alternative funding methods.

Criminal activities conducted for profit may range from local crimes of theft, burglary, and extortion to illicit trafficking of high-value commodities on a transnational scale. Terrorist groups may also "tax" other groups or charge a security or protection fee for permitting illicit trafficking activity to take place in a certain region under their control. Although terrorist groups may engage in criminal activity for fundraising, it is not always the case that such groups lose their ideological motivations. As one researcher explains, "[C]riminality does not imply criminalization. It is entirely possible for armed groups to exploit drugs, smuggling, and extortion without becoming motivated by these activities. Resources do not speak for themselves: simply engaging in criminality does not mean that an armed group exists to be criminal."[39]

The universe of potential crime-for-profit activities is vast. The following list describes three common transnational manifestations: drug trafficking, cigarette smuggling, and kidnapping-for-ransom.

- **Drug trafficking:** Illicit narcotics, particularly cocaine, heroin, hashish, and methamphetamine, as well as the chemical precursors required to manufacture such drugs, are attractive commodities to smuggle due to their high pecuniary value, as well as the ease with which they can be appropriated, processed, stored, and transported in small, difficult-to-detect movements and with limited static infrastructure costs. Terrorist groups are associated with major drug-producing countries, such as Afghanistan, Burma, Colombia, Morocco, and Peru, as well as among countries through which key drug transit routes pass.[40] In drug-producing countries, the narcotics trade has the potential to provide terrorist groups with an added bonus: recruits and sympathizers among impoverished, neglected, and isolated farmers who can not only cultivate drug crops but also popularize and reinforce anti-government movements.[41]

---

[39] Paul Staniland, "Organizing Insurgency: Networks, Resources, and Rebellion in South Asia," *International Security*, Vol. 37, No. 1 (Summer 2012), pp. 142-177.

[40] James A. Piazza, "The Opium Trade and Patterns of Terrorism in the Provinces of Afghanistan: An Empirical Analysis," *Terrorism and Political Violence*, Vol. 24, No. 2 (2012), pp. 213-234.

[41] Vanda Felbab-Brown, *Shooting Up: Counterinsurgency and the War on Drugs* (Washington, D.C.: Brookings Institution Press, 2010).

Afghan Drugs and the Taliban

As the single largest source of illicit opium and heroin worldwide for the past decade, the narcotics trade is both a major cause and consequence of criminality and insecurity in Afghanistan. Although historically not always the case, the opiate trade today appears to be one of several key sources of funds for the Taliban.[42] According to the U.N. Office on Drugs and Crime (UNODC), Afghan opiates generated approximately $68 billion in proceeds in 2009, of which some $140 million-$170 million went to anti-government insurgency groups, such as the Taliban.[43] U.S. reports further indicate that some of the Taliban's narcotics proceeds have been funneled in and out of Afghanistan and countries in the Persian Gulf through hawala-style informal value transfer networks and money exchanges houses, such as the New Ansari Money Exchange.[44]

Research indicates that the Taliban reportedly obtains drug-related proceeds in several ways.[45] Taliban commanders reportedly collect agricultural tithes (*ushr*) from poppy farmers and roadside levies (*zakat*) from traffickers. Additionally, the Taliban reportedly receives money, vehicles, and weapons in exchange for protection against interdiction and eradication.[46] The Taliban also supports efforts to facilitate seasonal migrant flows toward opium poppy farms for harvest. Opium traffickers pay the Taliban to transport narcotics throughout Afghanistan to neighboring nations.[47] Moreover, Taliban fighters appear to provide security for processing labs and for shipments of the chemicals needed to make heroin.[48] They also help drug lords fight Afghan government forces engaged in poppy eradication efforts. Moreover, local Taliban commanders have at times directly engaged in drug trafficking activities to supplement their incomes.[49]

- **Illicit tobacco trade:** The production, smuggling, and sale of tobacco products, including genuine and counterfeit cigarettes, is a lucrative form of financing for organized crime as well as terrorist groups, such as Hezbollah, Hamas, the Kurdistan Worker's Party (PKK), and the Real Irish Republican Army (RIRA).[50]

---

[42] In 2000, the Taliban implemented countrywide opium ban that resulted in the largest one-year reduction in opium poppy cultivation recorded by the United Nations. See also United Nations Office on Drugs and Crime (UNODC) and the World Bank, *Afghanistan's Drug Industry: Structure, Functioning, Dynamics, and Implications for Counter-Narcotics Policy*, Doris Buddenberg and William A. Byrd, eds., November 28, 2006.

[43] UNODC, *The Global Afghan Opium Trade: A Threat Assessment*, July 2011.

[44] U.S. Department of the Treasury, "Treasury Designates New Ansari Money Exchange," press release, February 18, 2011; Ginger Thompson and Alissa J. Rubin, "Sanctions Placed on Afghan Exchange," *The New York Times*, February 18, 2011.

[45] See for example Barnett R. Rubin and Jake Sherman, *Counter-Narcotics to Stabilize Afghanistan: The False Promise of Crop Eradication*, Center on International Cooperation, New York University, February 2008; Peters, *How Opium Profits the Taliban*, United States Institute of Peace (USIP), Peaceworks No. 62, August 2009; Peters, *Crime and Insurgency in the Tribal Areas of Afghanistan and Pakistan, Combating Terrorism Center*, Don Rassler, ed., Combating Terrorism Center (CTC) at West Point, harmony project, October 15, 2010.

[46] James Risen, "Propping Up a Drug Lord, Then Arresting Him," *The New York Times*, December 11, 2010; DOJ, "Haji Bagcho Sentenced to Life in Prison on Drug Trafficking and Narco-Terrorism Charges," press release, June 12, 2012; Ryan Evans, "The Micro-Level of Civil War: The Case of Central Helmand Province," *CTC Sentinel*, CTC at West Point, Vol. 5, Iss. 9 (September 2012), pp. 14-17.

[47] Julia Preston, "Afghan Arrested in New York Said to Be A Heroin Kingpin," *The New York Times*, April 26, 2005; "Warlord or Druglord?" *Time Magazine*, February 8, 2007; Benjamin Weiser, "In Drug Trial, Sharply Differing Portraits of Afghan With Ties to the Taliban," *The New York Times*, September 11, 2008.

[48] Theresa Cook, "Alleged Taliban-Linked Drug Trafficker Charged in U.S.," *ABC News*, May 11, 2007.

[49] DOJ, "Member of Afghan Taliban Sentenced to Life in Prison in Nation's First Conviction on Narco-Terror Charges," press release, December 22, 2008.

[50] U.S. District Court, Western District of North Carolina, Charlotte Division, *United States of America v Mohamad Youssef Hammoud et al.*, indictment, March 28, 2001; U.S. Department of Homeland Security (DHS), Immigration and Customs Enforcement (ICE), "Mohamad Youssef Hammoud Sentenced to 30 Years in Terrorism Financing Case," press release, January 27, 2011; Sari Horwitz, "Cigarette Smuggling Linked to Terrorism," *The Washington Post*, June 8, 2004; U.S. Congress, House Committee on Homeland Security, *Tobacco and Terror: How Cigarette Smuggling is Funding Our Enemies Abroad*, minority staff report, April 2008. U.S. General Accounting Office (GAO), *Terrorist Financing: U.S. Agencies Should Systematically Assess Terrorists' Use of Alternative Financing Mechanisms*, GAO- (continued...)

Cigarette smuggling schemes as a means for financing terrorists have been discovered in a range of countries and regions, including the United States, Europe, Turkey, the Middle East and North Africa, and Iraq. Criminals and terrorists may be drawn to the illicit tobacco trade to take advantage of price differentials across jurisdictions, bootlegging small consignments from a low-tax or duty-free outlet and re-selling the products elsewhere at a higher price. If sufficiently resourced, some groups may conduct larger-scale operations that divert and smuggle commercial-sized volumes, those in excess of 1 million cigarettes per consignment, for subsequent distribution and sale.

- **Kidnapping for ransom:** A form of hostage taking, kidnapping for ransom (KFR) is a popular means of collecting illicit profits for both organized crime as well as terrorist groups. KFR is often perceived as a crime of low risk, low cost, and high reward. As has reportedly been the case for groups such as AQIM, AQI, the Taliban, and ASG, a single ransom payment has the potential to cover several months of operating expenses.[51] According to the Financial Action Task Force (FATF), AQIM alone has collected at least $65 million (U.S. dollars) in KFR payments from 2005 through 2011—a significant portion of its annual budget, which is reported to total approximately 15 million Euros per year.[52] Authorities are particularly challenged to respond to KFR situations because they often take place in insecure, politically volatile locations that are difficult to control or access; involve third-party intermediaries who may facilitate negotiations of ransom payments without the approval and knowledge of government officials; and are characterized by opaque and difficult-to-track ransom payment transactions that involve both alternative remittance mechanisms and the formal international banking system.

Illicit Support Activity

Both criminal and terrorist groups rely on a variety of illicit support activities to further their operations. Although some such activities can be conducted with in-house capabilities and assets, others may require cooperation with external criminal specialists, corrupt "gatekeepers," local and regional "fixers," and "shadow facilitators."[53] The depth and durability of these crime-

---

(...continued)

04-163, November 2003; Maarten van Dijck, "The Link Between the Financing of Terrorism and Cigarette Smuggling. What Evidence is There? *HUMSEC Journal*, Vol. 1, Iss. 1 (June 2007), pp. 5-29; William Billingslea, "Illicit Cigarette Trafficking and the Funding of Terrorism," *The Police Chief*, Vol. 71, No. 2 (2004); Financial Action Task Force (FATF), *Illicit Tobacco Trade*, June 2012; Matthew Levitt, *Hamas: Politics, Charity, and Terrorism in the Service of Jihad* (New Haven: Yale University Press, 2006).

[51] Peters, *Crime and Insurgency in the Tribal Areas* ... , October 2010; Peters, *Haqqani Network Financing: The Evolution of an Industry*, CTC at West Point, harmony program, July 2012; Zia Ur Rehman, "Taliban Recruiting and Fundraising in Karachi," *CTC Sentinel*, CTC at West Point, Vol. 5, Iss. 7 (July 2012), pp. 9-11; McKenzie O'Brien, "Fluctuations Between Crime and Terror: The Case of Abu Sayyaf's Kidnapping Activities," *Terrorism and Political Violence*, Vol. 24, No. 2 (2012), pp. 320-336; FATF, *Organised Maritime Piracy and Related Kidnapping for Ransom*, July 2011; U.S. Department of the Treasury, "Remarks of Under Secretary David Cohen at Chatham house on 'Kidnapping for Ransom: The Growing Terrorist Financing Challenge,'" October 5, 2012.

[52] FATF, *Organised Maritime Piracy and Related Kidnapping for Ransom*, July 2011.

[53] Douglas Farah, *Fixers, Super Fixers and Shadow Facilitators: How Networks Connect*, International Assessment and Strategy Center, April 23, 2012; FATF, *Global Money Laundering and Terrorist Financing Threat Assessment*, July 2010; Shelley and Picarelli, "Methods Not Motives ... ," 2002.

terrorism relationships for support activities vary. Some terrorist groups view links to outside criminal networks as short-term marriages of convenience, where the actors build ephemeral business ties. These interactions often appear to be distinctly transactional in nature, with one criminal actor or organization providing a specific, tangible service to a terrorist group. In other cases, these relationships will be more synergistic, with terrorist and criminal groups creating enduring coalitions. In such coalition relationships, criminals and terrorists assume complementary but separate roles.

- **Money laundering:** Illicit support activities may include money laundering techniques to obfuscate the origins and recipients of funds through front companies, charities, shell corporations, and other third-party business structures. The movement and storage of money may also involve illicit support activities such as bulk cash smuggling and cash couriers; the exploitation of informal remittance mechanisms, international trade systems, and the formal international banking sector; and the use of unregulated diamonds, gold, and other minerals and commodities for stored value.[54]

---

[54] GAO, *Terrorist Financing ...* , November 2003; Rabasa et al., "Chapter Seven: The Convergence of Terrorism ... ," 2006. In the late 1990s and early 2000s, Al Qaeda purportedly used illegal diamond trade in Africa as a means of stored value transfer and as part of gems-for-weapons deals.

Hezbollah, Narcotics, and Illicit Finance: Global Interactions

Hezbollah is a Shiite Islamist militia, political party, and social welfare organization, as well as a State Department-listed FTO and a specially designated terrorist group pursuant to EOs 12947 and 13224.[55] According to official U.S. government statements, it derives financial benefits from a sprawling global commercial network of licit and illicit businesses that not only generates revenue for the organization but also provides numerous outlets through which illicit funds can be laundered, disguised, and moved (see also the "Hezbollah" section below, under "Organizational Evolution and Variation"). Although anecdotal reports have long appeared to connect Hezbollah global operations with drug trafficking, money laundering, and other illicit activity, several recent cases in 2011 have highlighted the potential transnational reach of Hezbollah's illicit finance activities.[56]

In February 2011, the Treasury Department's Financial Crimes Enforcement Network (FinCEN) designated Lebanese Canadian Bank SAL as a financial institution of primary money laundering concern pursuant to Section 311 of the USA PATRIOT Act (31 U.S.C. 5318A). In its public notice on the Section 311 finding, FinCEN described the Lebanese Canadian Bank SAL as "routinely used by drug traffickers and money launderers operating in various countries in Central and South America, Europe, Africa, and the Middle East" and that Hezbollah profited from the criminal activities of this global illicit financial network.[57]

Central to the designation were law enforcement and other sources of information that linked the Colombia-based narcotics trafficking kingpin Ayman Joumaa with a global network involving Hezbollah facilitators, such as Ali Mohamad Saleh, and other linked money laundering operations, including those controlled by Jorge Fadlallah Cheaitelly and Mohamad Zouheir El Khansa.[58] In January 2011, the Treasury Department designated Joumaa as a drug kingpin (SDNTs) and additionally identified him as a specially designated global terrorist (SDGT) in June 2012. In December 2011, Joumaa was also indicted on drug charges in the United States. According to such charges, he allegedly coordinated cocaine shipments in connection with the Mexican DTO Los Zetas and laundered as much as $200 million per month through accounts held with Lebanese Canadian Bank SAL and other financial institutions.[59] His South and Central American drug trafficking operations shipped cocaine to the United States and well as to West Africa for further distribution to Europe. Joumaa reportedly paid undisclosed fees to Hezbollah to facilitate the transportation and laundering of narcotics proceeds. For example, for bulk cash movements through Beirut International Airport, Joumaa paid Hezbollah security to safeguard and transport cash.

Joumaa also reportedly used trade-based money laundering (TBML) schemes to help conceal and disguise the true source, nature, ownership, and control of the narcotics proceeds. Such schemes involved Asian suppliers of consumer goods as well as used car dealerships in the United States. As part of the U.S. car sales-TBML scheme, for example, Hezbollah owned and controlled funds are transferred from Lebanon to the United States via banks, currency exchange houses, and individuals in order to purchase used cars. The cars would be shipped to West Africa and sold for cash. Cash proceeds, in turn, would be transferred to Lebanon through Hezbollah-linked bulk cash smugglers, hawaladars, and currency brokers.

Hezbollah's contacts in West Africa make this region in particular an attractive mid-point for exchanging contraband and cash and connecting with like-minded, ideologically driven criminals. In another recent U.S. narcotics trafficking case, for example, a West Africa-based criminal facilitator and member of the Free Patriotic Movement, a Lebanese Christian party aligned with Hezbollah in the Lebanese cabinet, reportedly provided extensive services to Hezbollah. According to his indictment, Maroun Saade would pay local bribes to release Hezbollah's cash couriers who were arrested in West Africa.[60] In the DEA-led operation that ultimately caught Saade and several of his associates, he agreed to provide individuals whom he thought were Taliban (though were in fact DEA confidential sources) with cocaine in exchange for weapons and heroin.

---

[55] For more on Hezbollah see CRS Report R41446, *Hezbollah: Background and Issues for Congress*, by Casey L. Addis and Christopher M. Blanchard.

[56] For other examples of Hezbollah's reported illicit activity see Nathan Vardi, "Hezbollah's Hoard," *Forbes*, August 14, 2006; Prepared testimony of Washington Institute for Near East Policy Senior Fellow and Director of Terrorism Studies Matthew Levitt, in U.S. Congress, Senate Committee on Homeland Security and Government Affairs, *Counterfeit Goods: Easy Cash for Criminals and Terrorists*, S.Hrg. 109-202, 109th Cong., 1st sess., May 25, 2005 (Washington, D.C.: U.S. Government Printing Office, 2005); Levitt, "Hizbullah Narco-Terrorism: A Growing Cross-Border Threat," *IHS Defense, Risk, and Security Consulting*, September 2012.

[57] U.S. Department of the Treasury, Financial Crimes Enforcement Network (FinCEN), "Finding that the Lebanese Canadian Bank SAL is a Financial Institution of Primary Money Laundering Concern," *Federal Register*, Vol. 76, No. 33 (February 17, 2011), pp. 9403-9406. See also Jo Becker, "Beirut Bank Seen as a Hub of Hezbollah's Financing." (continued...)

- **Illicit movements of people, arms, and equipment:** Other common forms of illicit support activities include the clandestine movement of people and the acquisition of materiel and communications equipment—all of which also require access to a variety of fraudulent international documents, including visas, passports, end user certificates, business registrations, shipping licenses, etc.[61] In one example, based on research conducted by the RAND Corporation and press reports, the Liberation Tigers of Tamil Eelam (LTTE) apparently maintain a cadre of criminal intermediaries for procuring and smuggling weapons. Such affiliations between arms brokers and the terrorist group appear to have been purposefully indirect in order to maintain sufficient distance between criminal activities and the leaders of the Tamil Tigers.[62] In another example, a traditional human smuggling network along the Syrian-Iraqi border was transformed by AQI into a key pathway used by foreign terrorists to clandestinely enter Iraq.[63]

(...continued)

The New York Times, December 13, 2011.

[58] DOJ, "U.S. Charges Alleged Lebanese Drug Kingpin With Laundering Drug Proceeds For Mexican And Colombian Drug Cartels," press release, December 13, 2011; U.S. Department of the Treasury, "Treasury Targets Key Panama-Based Money Laundering Operation Linked to Mexican and Colombian Drug Cartels," press release, December 29, 2011; U.S. Department of the Treasury, "Treasury Targets Major Money Laundering Network Linked to Drug Trafficker Ayman Joumaa and a Key Hizballah Supporter in South America," press release, June 27, 2012.

[59] U.S. District Court, Eastern District of Virginia, United States of America v Ayman Joumaa, indictment, November 23, 2011; U.S. District Court, SDNY, United States of America v Lebanese Canadian Bank SAL et al., complaint, December 15, 2011.

[60] U.S. District Court, SDNY, United States of America v Maroun Saade et al., indictment, unsealed February 14, 2011.

[61] *The 9/11 Commission Report: Final Report of the National Commission on Terrorist Attacks Upon the United States* (Washington, D.C.: U.S. Government Printing Office, 2004). See also Daveed Gartenstein-Ross and Kyle Dabruzzi, *The Convergence of Crime and Terror: Law Enforcement Opportunities and Perils*, Policing Terrorism Report No. 1, Center for Policing Terrorism at the Manhattan Institute, June 2007.

[62] Rabasa et al., "Chapter Seven: The Convergence of Terrorism ... ," 2006; DOJ, "Man Sentenced for Conspiracy to Provide Material Support to Terror Organization: Aided Tamil Tiger Terrorists in the Attempted Purchase of Surface to Air Missiles, Night Vision Devices, Machine Guns and State of the Art Firearms," press release, October 30, 2008; DOJ, "Singapore Man Sentenced to More than 4 Years in Prison for Conspiracy to Provide Material Support to a Foreign Terrorist Organization," press release, December 16, 2010.

[63] According to press accounts, Abu Ghadiyah (now deceased) and his family were reportedly long known to the U.S. intelligence community as a human smuggling network along the Syrian-Iraqi border. Around the time when U.S. forces invaded Baghdad in 2003, Abu Ghadiyah transformed his traditional smuggling operation into a key Al Qaeda in Iraq (AQI) hub for logistics and financial support—including provisions of passports, weapons, money, guides, and safe houses—to foreign terrorists seeking entry into Iraq. According to the Treasury Department, Abu Ghadiyah was appointed in 2004 as AQI's Syrian commander of logistics. In this position he not only continued his smuggling activities but also reportedly became involved in organizing at least two attacks in Iraq. See Mark Hosenball, "Targeting a 'Facilitator': A Commando Raid into Syria Aimed at Al Qaeda in Iraq," *Newsweek*, October 27, 2008; U.S. Department of the Treasury, "Treasury Designates Members of Abu Ghadiyah's Network: Facilitates Flow of Terrorists, Weapons, and Money From Syria to al Qaida in Iraq," press release, February 28, 2008; Matthew Levitt, "Al-Qa'ida's Finances: Evidence of Organizational Decline? *CTC Sentinel*, CTC at West Point, Vol. 1, Issue 5 (April 2008), pp. 7-9.

The Case of Victor Bout: Global Illicit Air Cargo Facilitator

Bout is believed to have been one of the world's most prodigious arms traffickers, notorious for his ability to transport practically anything anywhere with his fleet of airplanes, primarily former Soviet cargo planes. Prior to his arrest and eventual conviction in 2011, Bout was widely believed to have had a hand in a range of international contraband smuggling and sanctions-busting activities in Africa, southwest Asia, and elsewhere. Both the United Nations and the U.S. government sought to freeze his assets, and Belgium issued an arrest warrant for him in 2002 for crimes related to money laundering and diamond smuggling. He has also been accused of illegally transporting arms to the Taliban and Al Qaeda, while legally providing air freight transport around the world, including under contract for the U.S. military in Iraq.[64] He was caught in Thailand in 2008 in a DEA sting operation after attempting to sell surface-to-air missiles, AK-47s, ammunition, C-4 plastic explosives, and unmanned aerial vehicles to U.S. confidential sources purporting to be members of the FARC. Although Bout was ultimately extradited to the United States in November 2010, convicted in November 2011 on four counts, and sentenced to 25 years in prison in April 2012, other enterprising crime-terrorism facilitators may fill the vacuum he has left in the global illicit arms trade.[65]

- **Corruption:** Through bribery, financial inducements, and other forms of coercion, including the credible threat of violence, both criminal and terrorist elements can take advantage of corrupt actors to facilitate their operations and reduce the likelihood of detection and capture. Corrupt actors may range from border guards, financial regulators, justice sector officials, high-level policymakers and political figures, to private bankers, small business owners, and industry magnates. Government protection may take several forms, such as selectively ignoring evidence of illicit activity perpetrated by certain groups; actively providing intelligence and other support to illicit actors; or the wholesale ceding of authority and legitimacy to an illicit group.

Organizational Evolution and Variation

Typically, criminal groups are primarily driven by profit motives, whereas terrorist groups are ideologically driven. The motivations that drive terrorist and criminal groups, however, can evolve with time. A purely criminal group may transform to adopt political goals and ideological motivations. Terrorist groups, on the other hand, may shift toward criminality. For some terrorist groups, criminal activity remains secondary to ideological ambitions. For others, profit-making may surpass political aspirations as the dominant operating rationale. The level of involvement and expertise in terrorist or criminal activities may vary, depending on the organization's current leadership, membership composition, geographic distribution of sympathizers and diaspora networks, dependence on state sponsorship, and physical proximity or access to illicit resources.[66] Frequently cited terrorist organizations involved in criminal activity include, among others, ASG,

---

[64] See for example Michael Wines, "A Nation Challenged: A Suspect; Russian Goes on the Air to Deny Al Qaeda Ties," *The New York Times*, March 1, 2002; Peter Landesman, "Arms and the Man," *The New York Times Magazine*, August 17, 2003; Douglas Farah and Stephen Braun, *Merchant of Death: Money, Guns, Planes, and the Man Who Makes War Possible* (Hoboken, NJ: John Wiley & Sons, Inc., 2007); Nicholas Schmidle, "Disarming Viktor Bout," *The New Yorker*, March 5, 2012.

[65] DOJ, "Viktor Bout Extradited to the United States to Stand Trial on Terrorism Charges," press release, November 17, 2010; DOJ, "International Arms Dealer Viktor Bout Convicted in New York of Terrorism Crimes," press release, November 2, 2011; DOJ, "International Arms Dealer Viktor Bout Sentenced in Manhattan Federal Court to 25 Years in Prison for Terrorism Crimes," press release, April 5, 2012; Kathi Lynn Austin, *Viktor Bout's Gunrunning Successors: A Lethal Game of Catch Me If You Can*, Conflict Awareness Project, August 2012.

[66] See also Victor Asal, Kathleen Deloughery, and Brian J. Phillips, "When Politicians Sell Drugs: Examining Why Middle East Ethnopolitical Organizations Are Involved in the Drug Trade," *Terrorism and Political Violence*, Vol. 24, No. 2 (2012), pp. 199-212.

Al Qaeda's affiliates, D-Company, PKK, FARC, Haqqani Network, and Hezbollah. Brief descriptions of these groups' criminal activities are described below.

Abu Sayyaf Group (ASG)

A Philippines-based terrorist group, ASG appears to have at times prioritized criminal activities over ideological operations. Major shifts toward crime occurred in conjunction with leadership and membership composition changes, which altered the relative importance of ideological zeal and criminal tendencies.

> **Further CRS Reading**
>
> For more information on ASG and other internal security threats in the Philippines, see CRS Report RL33233, *The Republic of the Philippines and U.S. Interests*, by Thomas Lum.

During its periods of high criminality, ASG became well known for its success in kidnappings for ransom, maritime piracy, and arms trafficking.[67] Observers suggest that the group's overall drive toward criminal activity has been perpetuated by the group's ability to generate illicit profits, with new recruits tending to be more motivated by ASG's promise of financial wealth rather than ideological convictions. The State Department has listed ASG as an FTO since 1997, and President George W. Bush designated ASG a specially designated global terrorist (SDGT) pursuant to EO 13224 in 2001.

Al Qaeda's Affiliates

There is no conclusive evidence of senior-level Al Qaeda members directly involved with or motivated by organized crime. Many speculate that this is because of the group's strict ideological beliefs and fear of a loss of credibility if senior leaders were found to be directly involved in such activities. Connections to organized crime activity, however, can be drawn among mid-level

> **Further CRS Reading**
>
> For background information on the global reach of Al Qaeda, see archived CRS Report R41070, *Al Qaeda and Affiliates: Historical Perspective, Global Presence, and Implications for U.S. Policy*, coordinated by John Rollins.

and low-level Al Qaeda members and supporters. Moreover, it appears that Al Qaeda's affiliates and franchises do not necessarily share the same aversion to criminal activity. Notable crime-funded Al Qaeda affiliates include AQIM and AQI.[68] Additionally, Al Qaeda's disinclination toward direct involvement in organized crime has not prevented it from cooperating, supporting, and jointly training with other insurgent groups that are more entrenched in trafficking and smuggling activities, including the Haqqani Network and the Taliban. The State Department designated Al Qaeda as an FTO in October 1999, and President George W. Bush designated it as an SDGT pursuant to EO 13224 in 2001. Several of its affiliates have also been designated separately as FTOs, including AQI in December 2004, AQIM in February 2008 (AQIM was also previously designated in March 2002 when it was called the Salafist Group for Call and Combat, GSPC), and AQAP in January 2010.

---

[67] McKenzie O'Brien, "Fluctuations Between Crime and Terror: The Case of Abu Sayyaf's Kidnapping Activities," *Terrorism and Political Violence*, Vol. 24, No. 2 (2012), pp. 320-336. See also Rabasa et al., "Chapter Seven: The Convergence of Terrorism ... ," 2006.

[68] U.S. Department of State, *Country Reports on Terrorism 2011*, July 2012; U.S. Department of the Treasury, "Remarks of Under Secretary David Cohen at Chatham house on 'Kidnapping for Ransom: The Growing Terrorist Financing Challenge,'" October 5, 2012.

The 2004 Madrid Bombing and Its Connections to Drugs

The Al Qaeda cell that committed the March 2004 train bombings in Madrid provides an example of terrorist cell whose members used extensive criminal endeavors to fund its operations. One of the plot's ringleaders and several accomplices were drug dealers and traffickers before they became radicalized and joined the Madrid cell. These operatives sold narcotics to pay for cars, safe houses, phones, and other logistical support, and weapons. Furthermore, they reportedly exchanged drugs for the explosives used in the attacks.[69] One of the masterminds of the Madrid bombings was reportedly Jamal Ahmidan, a major drug dealer who ran a far-reaching narcotics ring that sold hashish and Ecstasy throughout Western Europe in the 1990s. Ahmidan appears to have first become interested in extremist Islamic ideology while serving time in a Spanish prison in 1998, and then was fully radicalized in a Moroccan jail from 2000 to 2003.[70]

D-Company

Dawood Ibrahim, the alleged leader of D-Company, is an INTERPOL fugitive and wanted in connection with the 1993 Mumbai bombing and sanctioned under U.N. Security Council Resolution 1267. Ibrahim was listed in October 2003 by the Treasury Department as a specially designated global terrorist (SDGT), and both Ibrahim and his organization were listed as significant foreign narcotics traffickers (SDNTKs) in May 2008, pursuant to the Foreign Narcotics Kingpin Designation Act. His organization, D-Company, can be characterized as both a transnational criminal syndicate as well as ideologically aligned with terrorist groups operating in South Asia, including Lashkar-e-Taiba (LeT). According to reports, D-Company originated as a smuggling operation in the 1970s. It evolved in the 1990s into an organized crime group not only motivated by profit but also one that engaged in insurgent activity, eventually supporting efforts to smuggle weapons to militant and terrorist groups in the region. By the 1990s, it began to conduct and participate in terrorist attacks, including the March 12, 1993, Bombay bombing. D-Company's criminal activities reportedly span extortion, smuggling, narcotics trafficking, and contract killings.[71] Its apparent willingness to work with and provide logistical, financial, and material support to ideologically motivated violent groups exemplifies the risks associated with converged criminal and terrorists threats.[72]

Kurdistan Worker's Party (PKK)

Formed in the 1970s and operational since the early 1980s as a Kurdish nationalist group with Marxist-Leninist leanings, the PKK increasingly turned to crime after it lost its state sponsors.[73] By the late 1990s, and particularly after its leader Abdullah Ocalan was captured in 1999, the

---

[69] Dale Fuchs, "Spain Says Bombers Drank Water From Mecca and Sold Drugs," *The New York Times*, April 15, 2004; "Madrid Bombing Probe Finds No al-Qaida Link: Two-Year Investigation Concludes that Terrorists Were Homegrown Radicals," *Associated Press*, March 9, 2006.

[70] Andrea Elliott, "Where Boys Grow Up to Be Jihadis," *The New York Times*, November 25, 2007; Sebastian Rotella, "Jihad's Unlikely Alliance," *Los Angeles Times*, Mary 23, 2004; Phil Williams, "In Cold Blood: The Madrid Bombings," *Perspectives on Terrorism*, Vol. 2, No. 9 (2008).

[71] Sumita Sarkar and Arvind Tiwari, "Combating Organised Crime: A Case Study of Mumbai City," *Faultlines*, Vol. 12, Art. 5 (2002); Gregory F. Treverton et al., *Film Piracy, Organized Crime, and Terrorism*, RAND Corporation, 2009; "Bad Company: South Asia's Regional Criminal Organisation," *Jane's Intelligence Review*, August 2009; Gilbert King, *The Most Dangerous Man in the World: Dawood Ibrahim* (New York, NY: Camberlain Bros., 2004).

[72] Ben Riley and Kathleen Kiernan (Kiernan Group Holdings), eds., *The 'New' Face of Transnational Criminal Organizations (TCOs): A Geopolitical Perspective and Implications to U.S. National Security*, March 2013.

[73] Its state sponsors included Syria, which hosted the group's leadership, as well as the Soviet Union, Iran, Iraq, and Greece.

PKK invested heavily in transnational organized crime activities, such as drug trafficking, arms smuggling, human smuggling, extortion, money laundering, counterfeiting, and illegal cigarettes. By the 1990s, the PKK had formed specialized units to variously carry out militant operations, contraband trafficking, political activities, and information campaigns.[74] As a result, some parts of the PKK appear to behave more like a criminal organization rather than a terrorist or guerrilla organization.[75] According to the U.S. government, many of these criminal activities are centered in Europe, where there is a significant Kurdish diaspora population. The State Department designated the PKK as an FTO in October 1997. The PKK was also designated as an SDGT in 2001. For its alleged involvement in drug trafficking, the President designated the PKK as an SDNTK in May 2008, pursuant to the Foreign Narcotics Kingpin Designation Act.

Revolutionary Armed Forces of Colombia (FARC)

Operational since the 1960s, the FARC has been described as one of the largest, oldest, most violent, and best-equipped terrorist organization in Latin America. Its longevity is due in part to its involvement in the drug trade. The enormous profit opportunity that drug trafficking has provided to the FARC is widely viewed as the driving factor for its involvement in such criminal activity. According to reports, the FARC first became

> **Further CRS Reading**
>
> For more on the FARC, see CRS Report RS21049, *Latin America: Terrorism Issues*, by Mark P. Sullivan and June S. Beittel, and CRS Report RL32250, *Colombia: Background, U.S. Relations, and Congressional Interest*, by June S. Beittel.

involved in the drug trade in the 1980s by levying protection fees on coca bush harvesters, buyers of coca paste and cocaine base, and cocaine processing laboratory operators in territory under FARC control. Over time, the FARC took a more direct role in drug production and distribution. By the 2000s, the FARC had reportedly become the world's largest supplier of cocaine. The FARC also reportedly generates revenue from extortion rackets, kidnapping ransoms, and illegal mining.[76] Exploratory peace talks between the Colombian government and the FARC began in August 2012, the outcome of which may have implications for the FARC's future involvement in illicit criminal activities. The State Department designated the FARC as an FTO in October 1997.

---

[74] Abdulkadir Onay, *PKK Criminal Networks and Fronts in Europe*, The Washington Institute for Near East Policy, Policy Watch Report No. 1344, February 21, 2008; Vera Eccarius-Kelly, "Surreptitious Lifelines: A Structural Analysis of the FARC and the PKK," *Terrorism and Political Violence*, Vol. 24, No. 2 (2012), pp. 235-258; "Partiya Karkeren Kurdistan (PKK), *Jane's World Insurgency and Terrorism*, August 2012.

[75] Since the 2003 U.S.-led invasion of Iraq, the PKK has used safe havens in northern Iraq to coordinate and launch attacks against Turkish targets. PKK violence also appears to have resurged during the early stages of the "Arab Spring" and particularly following the outbreak of civil conflict in Syria. Some reports speculate that the Asad regime and Iran might be providing political and/or material support to these groups.

[76] Rex A. Hudson et al., *A Global Overview of Narcotics-Funded Terrorist and Other Extremist Groups*, Library of Congress, Federal Research Division, May 2002; Eccarius-Kelly, "Surreptitious Lifelines ... ," 2012; U.S. Department of State, *Country Reports on Terrorism 2011*, July 2012. It is also believed to have entered into strategic alliances with external criminal syndicates and other terrorist organizations. The FARC, for example, reportedly maintains contacts with Russian, Ukrainian, Croatian, and Jordanian crime families, and armed groups in more than a dozen foreign countries, for the purposes of supplying the FARC with weapons and communications equipment. The FARC also allegedly collaborates with other terrorist groups, including Basque Homeland and Freedom (ETA) and a smaller insurgent group in Colombia, the National Liberation Army (ELN).

Haqqani Network

The family-run Haqqani Network is commonly described as an insurgent group, in equal measures one of the Taliban's most capable militant factions as well as an enterprising transnational criminal organization. Headquartered in North Waziristan, Pakistan, this insurgent group is suspected of conducting major attacks against allied coalition members of the North Atlantic Treaty Organization (NATO) and U.S. forces in

> **Further CRS Reading**
>
> For more information on Haqqani Network attacks, background, and political implications, see CRS Report R41832, *Pakistan-U.S. Relations*, by K. Alan Kronstadt, and CRS Report RL30588, *Afghanistan: Post-Taliban Governance, Security, and U.S. Policy*, by Kenneth Katzman.

Afghanistan as well as active involvement in a wide range of highly profitable licit and illicit activity. In the 1980s, Jalaluddin Haqqani first gained a reputation as an effective mujahedin commander and U.S. ally against the Soviet Union. He later joined the Taliban regime in the 1990s when in power in Afghanistan. The group continues to maintain relationships not only with Al Qaeda and other militant groups in the region, but also purportedly benefits from a relationship with Pakistan's Inter-Services Intelligence Directorate (ISI)—a relationship strongly decried by America's top ranking military officer in September 2011. As part of a strategy of financial diversification to ensure the organization's resiliency against external pressures, the group also benefits financially from extortion and protection rackets, robbery schemes, kidnapping for ransom, and contraband smuggling (e.g., drugs, precursor chemicals, timber, and chromite).[77] The Haqqanis also reportedly control licit import-export, transportation, real estate, and construction firms through which illicit proceeds can be laundered. Pursuant to the Haqqani Network Terrorist Designation Act of 2012 (P.L. 112-168), the State Department designated the group as an FTO in September 2012.

Hezbollah

Based in Lebanon, with established cells in Africa, North and South America, Asia, and Europe, Hezbollah is known to have or suspected of having been involved in terrorist attacks against U.S. interests worldwide. Although primarily funded and trained with support from state sponsors, chiefly Iran, Hezbollah also

> **Further CRS Reading**
>
> For more on Hezbollah, see CRS Report R41446, *Hezbollah: Background and Issues for Congress*, by Casey L. Addis and Christopher M. Blanchard.

reportedly benefits from a sprawling global commercial network of licit and illicit businesses, largely connected to expatriate Lebanese communities worldwide.[78] Sources of funds include private donors and large-scale investments in legitimate businesses. Criminal indictments and statements by U.S. officials and other experts suggest that Hezbollah has also become well-integrated in the domain of transnational organized crime, deriving profits from a wide range of illicit enterprises, such as drug trafficking, precursor chemical trafficking, counterfeit

---

[77] David Rhode, "Held By the Taliban," *The New York Times*, November 17, 2009; Jeffrey A. Dressler, *The Haqqani Network: From Pakistan to Afghanistan*, Institute for the Study of War, Afghanistan Report No. 6, October 2010; Alissa Rubin and James Risen, "Costly Afghanistan Road Project is Marred by Unsavory Alliances," *The New York Times*, May 1, 2011; Mark Mazzetti, Scott Shane, and Alissa J. Rubin, "Brutal Haqqani Crime Clan Bedevils U.S. in Afghanistan," *The New York Times*, September 24, 2011; Peters, *Haqqani Network Financing: The Evolution of an Industry*, CTC at West Point, harmony project, July 2012; U.S. Department of State, *Report to Congress as Required by The Haqqani Network Terrorist Designation Act of 2012*, September 7, 2012; U.S. Congress, House Committee on Foreign Affairs, Subcommittee on Terrorism, Nonproliferation, and Trade, *Combating the Haqqani Terrorist Network*, 112th Cong., 2nd sess., September 13, 2012.

[78] U.S. Department of State, *Country Reports on Terrorism 2011*, July 2012.

---

pharmaceutical trafficking, sales of counterfeit commercial goods and electronics, auto theft and fraudulent re-sale, diamond smuggling, cigarette and baby formula smuggling, credit card fraud, and insurance scams, among potentially many others.[79] Pursuant to EO 12947, Hezbollah was designated in January 1995 as a specially designated terrorist (SDT). The State Department designated Hezbollah as an FTO in 1997. In October 2001, Hezbollah was also designated as an SDGT pursuant to EO 13224.

Foreign Policy Responses

With recognition that every crime-terrorism partnering circumstance will be different and the tools to identify and address such concerns may change, a wide range of anti-crime and counterterrorism policy options can be considered. The variety of options available, however, also challenges policymakers to consider several key questions in formulating responses. Should a specific agency or an interagency coordinating body be designated as leading U.S. government responses to crime-terrorism threats? Under what circumstances would U.S. responses to crime-terrorism threats be most appropriately led by the intelligence community, military, diplomatic corps, or law enforcement agencies? How can resources and authorities be allocated and managed to avoid excessive duplication while also ensuring effective policy response coverage?

The following sections describe selected key foreign policy responses to crime-terrorism nexus threats and related policy considerations for Congress for each response. These may be applied in various combinations or sequences, depending on the specific circumstances.

Diplomacy

U.S. diplomatic efforts to promote anti-crime and counterterrorism goals occur through bilateral, regional, and multilateral mechanisms. Such efforts are often led by the U.S. Department of State and include initiatives developed by its regional bureaus, the Bureau for International Narcotics and Law Enforcement Affairs (INL), and the Bureau of Counterterrorism (CT). Relevant U.N. treaties to which the United States is party to include the International Convention Against the Taking of Hostages, International Convention for the Suppression of Terrorist Bombings, International Convention for the Suppression of the Financing of Terrorism, U.N. Convention against Transnational Organized Crime, and International Convention for the Suppression of Acts

---

[79] In one example of Hezbollah-linked crime-terrorism activity within the United States, a group of individuals in Pennsylvania, purportedly at the request of a member of Hezbollah's political bureau in Beirut, Lebanon, sought to provide material support to Hezbollah in the form of weapons as well as counterfeit and stolen cash generated from trafficking in a wide range of counterfeit goods, such as fake passports, cell phones, computers, gaming systems, cars, and designer sports jerseys. See DOJ, "Four Indicted for Conspiring to Support Hizballah; Six Others Charged with Related Crimes," press release, November 24, 2009; Hitha Prabhakar, *Black Market Billions: How Organized Retail Crime Funds Global Terrorists* (Upper Saddle River, NJ: FT Press, 2012); Prepared testimony of Washington Institute for Near East Policy Director of the Stein Program on Counterterrorism and Intelligence Matthew Levitt, in U.S. Congress, House Homeland Security Committee, *Iran, Hezbollah, and the Threat to the Homeland*, 112th Cong., 2nd sess., March 21, 2012. See also U.S. Department of State, *Country Reports on Terrorism 2012*, May 2013; Rabasa et al., "Chapter Seven: The Convergence of Terrorism ... ," 2006; Doug Farah, *Hezbollah's External Support Network in West Africa and Latin America*, International Assessment and Strategy Center, August 4, 2006; Prepared testimony of U.S. Department of State Principal Deputy Coordinator of the Office of the Coordinator for Counterterrorism Frank C. Urbancic, Jr., in U.S. Congress, House Committee on International Relations, Subcommittee on International Terrorism and Nonproliferation and Subcommittee on Middle East and Central Asia, *Hizballah's Global Reach*, Serial No. 109-233, 109th Cong., 2nd sess., September 28, 2006.

of Nuclear Terrorism. Through the U.N. Security Council, the United States also participates in the Security Council Sanctions Committee. The Sanctions Committee administers and enforces a range of sanctions and targeted measures against Al Qaeda and the Taliban, among others, which include arms embargoes, travel bans, asset freezes, and diplomatic restrictions.

Bilaterally, the U.S. government maintains mutual legal assistance treaties (MLATs) and extradition agreements with foreign countries to facilitate transnational investigations and information sharing. Other options available to the State Department include designating entities as FTOs, pursuant to the Immigration and Nationality Act (INA), as amended, and barring known foreign terrorists and transnational organized criminals from entry into the United States and providing grounds to remove and deport such individuals if in the United States, pursuant to several visa ineligibility conditions.[80] (See text box below for more on a recent FTO designation, the Haqqani Network.) Additionally, the U.S. Department of the Treasury's Office of Terrorist Financing and Financial Crimes (TFFC) leads the U.S. delegation in meetings of the Financial Action Task Force (FATF), an international body that develops global regulatory standards for combating money laundering and terrorist financing.

Congress has provided direction to relevant federal departments to conduct diplomatic activities to address crime-terrorism issues by enacting legislation that authorizes and appropriates funds to relevant agencies to perform such tasks, as well as by conducting program oversight through hearings and reporting requirements. Given the inherently transnational nature of many current crime-terrorism challenges, diplomacy often plays a central role in responses. The extent to which diplomacy can be effective in combating crime-terrorism threats, however, is limited by delays associated with achieving consensus agreements and potentially long-lasting gaps in foreign political will and capacity.

---

[80] For further discussion of criminal aliens, see CRS Report RL32480, *Immigration Consequences of Criminal Activity*, by Michael John Garcia. Pursuant to authorities under the INA, as amended, President Obama issued Presidential Proclamation (PP) 8693, which elaborated on existing travel prohibitions against specially designated terrorists and transnational organized criminals. See President Barack Obama, "Proclamation 8693 of July 24, 2011: Suspension of Entry of Aliens Subject to United Nations Security Council Travel Bans and International Emergency Economic Powers Act Sanctions," *Federal Register*, Vol. 76, No. 144, pp. 44751-44755.

Designating the Haqqani Network

As discussed above, the Haqqani Network is a militant faction of the Taliban, whose insurgent activities include acts of terrorism as well as extensive involvement in transnational criminal activity. Although several senior members of the group had previously been listed by the Treasury Department as SDGTs, the Haqqani Network was not designated an FTO until September 2012. Congress contributed to its designation as an FTO with the passage of the Haqqani Network Terrorist Designation Act 2012 (S. 1959/H.R. 6036). Enacted on August 10, 2012 (P.L. 112-168), the act established that it was the sense of Congress that the Haqqani Network met the criteria for designation as an FTO pursuant to Section 219 of the Immigration and Nationality Act (INA) and that the Secretary of State should designate the group as such. The act required that the Secretary of State report to appropriate congressional committees within 30 days of enactment of the act with a detailed report on whether the Haqqani Network fit the description of FTOs. On September 7, 2012, the State Department transmitted its report to Congress, concluding that the Haqqani Network met the criteria for designation as an FTO: according to the State Department, it is a "foreign organization that engages in terrorism" and that its terrorist activity "threatens the security of U.S. nationals and the national security of the United States."

Foreign Assistance

Several U.S. departments and agencies administer programs to train foreign law enforcement officials and other security forces; develop legal frameworks in partner nations to criminalize and combat various crime-, drug-, and terrorism-related activities; and support institutional capacity building for foreign internal security and border enforcement entities. U.S. foreign assistance efforts to combat international terrorism or transnational crime can have mutually beneficial implications. In cases of crime-terrorism confluence, some have cautioned that an increasingly blurred line between counterterrorism and anti-crime assistance could reduce foreign aid transparency and raise additional challenges in planning and coordinating projects to avoid redundancy. In some cases, foreign development aid may also risk unintentionally providing illicit groups with an additional source of funding. In regions where known crime-terrorist groups are known to operate, such as Afghanistan, funds intended for development projects have at times benefited illicit groups, who offer development contractors with security and protection services.[81]

Most U.S. foreign police assistance is administered through the U.S. Departments of State and Defense, and programs are variously implemented by other U.S. agencies and federal contractors in host nations. In some situations, the U.S. government may be requested to support foreign militaries in their efforts to combat crime-terrorism threats, such as the FARC in Colombia or the Taliban in Afghanistan. In addition to U.S.-funded foreign security forces support efforts, the U.S. Agency for International Development (USAID) is often involved in developing related justice sector and rule of law assistance programs. DOJ maintains in-house expertise through its Office of Overseas Prosecutorial Development Assistance and Training (OPDAT) and International Criminal Investigative Training Assistance Program (ICITAP) to implement capacity building projects that support foreign countries investigate and prosecute cases involving transnational crime and international terrorism. U.S. federal prosecutors may serve as Resident Legal Advisors (RLAs) overseas to support related justice sector training, institution building, and legislative drafting.

---

[81] For one example in Afghanistan that may have resulted in development aid diverted to the Haqqani Network among other local militant groups, see Alissa J. Rubin and James Risen, "Costly Afghanistan Road Project is Marred by Unsavory Alliances," *The New York Times*, May 1, 2011.

Congress has played an active role in establishing the scope and amount of U.S. assistance that can be provided for the purposes of counterterrorism and anti-crime. Specific authorities are outlined in the Foreign Assistance Act of 1961, as amended, Title 10 of the U.S. Code, and periodic National Defense Authorization Acts. Additional conditions may also be included in appropriations acts for the various agencies involved in administering foreign assistance for counterterrorism and anti-crime.

Financial Actions

Several unilateral and multilateral policy mechanisms are available to block transactions and freeze assets of specified terrorist or criminal entities, as well as to strengthen international financial systems through enhanced regulatory requirements. Unilaterally, the Treasury Department's Office of Foreign Assets Control (OFAC) administers and enforces unilateral targeted financial sanctions against a list of foreign entities and individuals (specially designated nationals, or SDNs) that include SDGTs, FTOs, Middle Eastern terrorist organizations found to undermine and threaten Middle East peace process efforts (specially designated terrorists, or SDTs), transnational criminal organizations (TCOs), and specially designated narcotics traffickers and trafficking kingpins (SDNTs and SDNTKs). Authorities for OFAC to designate such entities are derived from executive order and legislative statutes, which include the International Emergency Economic Powers Act (EEPA), the Antiterrorism and Effective Death Penalty Act of 1996 (AEDPA), and the Foreign Narcotics Kingpin Designation Act.

Additionally, Title II of the USA PATRIOT ACT of 2001 (P.L. 108-56, as amended) introduced several policy tools that strengthened the existing U.S. framework to combat illicit finance. Among other provisions, this act developed a procedure, popularly known as Section 311, to apply enhanced regulatory requirements, called "special measures," against designated jurisdictions, financial institutions, and international transactions that are found to be involved in criminal or terrorist financing activities.[82] At the multilateral level, the United Nations administers several sanctions programs to freeze funds related to persons involved in acts of terrorism, including individuals and entities associated with Al Qaeda and the Taliban, pursuant to U.N. Security Council Resolution 1373 (2001), U.N. Security Council Resolution 1267 (1999), and U.N. Security Council Resolution 1988 (2011).

Many observers have argued that a key tool to combat the confluence of crime and terrorism is to follow their overlapping money trails and apply financial sanctions and heightened regulatory conditions to vulnerable financial sectors. Both types of groups require funds to sustain operations, and such funds often intersect with the formal international banking system. Critics of such tools to counter illicit financial transaction suggest that they are often laborious and time-intensive to implement, and not necessarily effective in dismantling crime or terrorism networks. Policymakers have acknowledged that criminals and terrorists continue to exploit opportunities to move funds and hide their financial tracks in multiple ways: in the formal financial system; through centuries-old techniques such as bulk cash smuggling, trade-based money laundering, and hawala-type informal value transfer systems; and through modern technologies such as pre-paid cards, mobile banking systems, and the Internet.

---

[82] Also highlighting the Treasury Department's awareness in the aftermath of September 11 that both criminals and terrorists seek to exploit the international financial system, it established in 2004 the Office of Intelligence and Analysis (OIA), now a formal member of the intelligence community.

Intelligence

Although few details are publicly available about the intelligence community's role in combating crime-terrorism threats, intelligence can play a significant role in developing strategic analyses that prioritize crime-terrorism trends of national security significance, as well as in developing operational and tactical responses to detect, influence, and target specific crime-terrorism networks, nodes, plans, and actors. The 2009 *National Intelligence Strategy* described the nexus between terrorism and criminal activities as among the intelligence community's priorities.

In the past, some have suggested that there appeared to be limited, if any, systematic gathering of intelligence related to the nexus between crime and terrorism and, as a result, an incomplete understanding of the scope and nature of relationships between and convergence among terrorists and criminal actors. The Obama Administration's 2011 *Strategy to Combat Transnational Organized Crime* acknowledged that "a shift in U.S. intelligence collection priorities" since 9/11 resulted in "significant gaps" related to transnational organized crime.[83] The 2011 Strategy also identified the enhancement of "U.S. intelligence collection, analysis, and counterintelligence" on transnational organized crime as "a necessary first step." Since 9/11, numerous bills have addressed terrorism as well a transnational crime-related issues. Similarly, a number of congressional hearings have focused on issues relating to international terrorism and transnational crime. Some observers suggest that heightened congressional focus on the confluence of crime and terrorism may have an impact on the executive branch's approach to the issue and appreciation for the risks and vulnerabilities associated with crime-terrorism partnering arrangements.

Military Actions

In some cases, particularly in non-permissive security environments in which traditional law enforcement units may have difficulty operating, the U.S. military has been called upon to contribute to certain joint counternarcotics and counterterrorism or counterinsurgency activities. In 2002, for example, Congress first authorized DOD to support a "unified campaign against narcotics trafficking ... [and] activities by organizations designated as terrorist organizations such as the Revolutionary Armed Forces of Colombia (FARC), the National Liberation Army (ELN), and the United Self-Defense Forces of Colombia (AUC)."[84] Although Congress renewed this authority through FY2012 in the National Defense Authorization Act for Fiscal Year 2012 (P.L. 112-81), it has not been codified and is limited only to activities in Colombia. Military operations in Afghanistan provide another example in which DOD has taken an expanded approach to crime-terrorism nexus issues. In late 2008, DOD amended its rules of engagement in Afghanistan to allow U.S. military commanders to target drug traffickers and others who provide material support to insurgent or terrorist groups such as the Taliban and members of hybrid crime-terrorism groups such as the Haqqani Network.[85] DOD further clarified that the U.S. military may accompany and provide force protection in counternarcotics field operations.[86] In some cases, the

---

[83] Obama Administration, *Strategy to Combat Transnational Organized Crime*, July 2011.

[84] Section 305 of P.L. 107-206.

[85] James Risen, "U.S. to Hunt Down Afghan Drug Lords Tied to Taliban," *The New York Times*, August 9, 2009.

[86] GAO, *Afghanistan Drug Control: Strategy Evolving and Progress Reported, but Interim Performance Targets and Evaluation of Justice Reform Efforts Needed*, GAO-10-291, March 2010.

U.S. military has chosen to take lethal action to rescue or attempt to rescue hostages in kidnapping for ransom situations.[87]

U.S. military involvement in situations where there are overlaps between anti-crime and counterterrorism goals is not necessarily warranted or desired. In some situations, political sensitivities and rules of engagement may prevent or prohibit the U.S. Armed Forces from direct involvement. Some observers caution that militarized counternarcotics or anti-crime policies may risk escalating suppression tactics and contribute to violations of human rights.

Investigations

Various elements of the U.S. Departments of Justice (DOJ) and the Department of Homeland Security (DHS) are tasked with investigating cases that involve alleged prohibited acts related to international terrorism and transnational crime. These include the U.S. Federal Bureau of Investigation (FBI), the U.S. Drug Enforcement Administration (DEA), the International Organized Crime Intelligence and Operations Center (IOC-2), and Immigration and Customs Enforcement (ICE). The State Department, DOD, and FBI also publicize rewards programs for citizen tips that lead to the apprehension of selected high-profile perpetrators of transnational organized crime, including money launderers, human traffickers, and drug traffickers, as well as terrorists.[88]

Some observers see the nexus between crime and terrorism as a potential benefit for detection and law enforcement prosecution that could be further exploited. Even if prosecutors do not have sufficient evidence to convict a suspected terrorist of terrorism-related charges, other criminal charges may be effectively used. Furthermore, some criminal charges, such as violations related to drug trafficking, can lead to jail sentences and penalties similar in magnitude to terrorism ones. It remains unclear, however, how effective such law enforcement and prosecution approaches have been to combat terrorism or how frequently such strategies have been implemented in practice, both in the United States and among partner nations, due to the lack of consistency in tracking cases with crime-terrorism nexus connections. Congress may have an interest in assessing how existing statutes have been used to support investigative and prosecution-related activities in response to entities suspected of engaging in terrorism-crime partnering activities. Assessing investigative, prosecution, and sentencing data collected in the 11 years since the attacks of 9/11 may provide Congress with information regarding statutes that have been effectively used to address crime-terrorism partnering activities and areas where additional legislative assistance might be required.

---

[87] In January 2012, for example, U.S. special forces reportedly rescued two hostages in Somalia, killing all nine kidnappers. In another instance, from February 2011, U.S. special forces attempted to rescue four hostages off the coast of Somalia, but their captors, reportedly Somali pirates, killed or fatally wounded all four before they could be rescued. Jeffrey Gettleman, Eric Schmitt, and Thom Shanker, "U.S. Swoops in to Free 2 from Pirates in Somali Raid," *The New York Times*, January 25, 2012; Adam Nagourney and Gettleman, "Pirates Brutally End Yachting Dream," *The New York Times*, February 22, 2011.

[88] In early January 2013, the 112th Congress enacted the Department of State Rewards Program Update and Technical Corrections Act of 2012 (P.L. 112-283). Prior to its enactment, the State Department's rewards programs were limited to offering payments for information leading to the arrest or conviction of individuals involved in major narcotics trafficking or international terrorism.

Investigation and Enforcement of International Narcoterrorism Cases

Section 122 of the USA PATRIOT Improvement and Reauthorization Act of 2005 (P.L. 109-177) added a new prohibition against narco-terrorism with enhanced criminal penalties. This provision, codified at 21 U.S.C. 960a, makes it a violation of U.S. law to engage in narcotics-related crimes anywhere in the world while knowing, conspiring, or intending to provide support, directly or indirectly, for a terrorist act or to a terrorist organization. In order to pursue these complex, transnational narco-terrorism cases against high-level, often foreign or foreign-located targets, DEA established the Counter-Narco-Terrorism Operations Center within its Special Operations Division (SOD) to manage its worldwide activities. In some countries, such as in Afghanistan, narco-terrorism operations are implemented on the ground through Foreign-Deployed Advisory and Support Teams (FAST) that collaborate on joint investigations together with host country counterparts.

There have been several publicly reported investigations and prosecutions involving alleged violations of 21 U.S.C. 960a. Such cases have involved individuals allegedly affiliated with groups, such as the Taliban, the United Self-Defense Forces of Colombia (AUC), Al Qaeda, Hezbollah, and the FARC.

International narco-terrorism prosecutions appear to have gained prominence since enactment of the USA PATRIOT Improvement and Reauthorization Act of 2005. For example, the Office of the U.S. Attorney for the Southern District of New York internally restructured its organizational units in January 2010 and merged its Terrorism and National Security Unit with its International Narcotics Trafficking Unit. This internal reorganization was designed to facilitate greater coordination with DEA on narco-terrorism cases. Explaining the apparent increased emphasis on narco-terrorism, the U.S. Attorney for the Southern District of New York stated:

> Since January 2010, this Office, in partnership with the DEA, has focused its attention even more closely on the serious threat that narco-terrorism poses to our national security. Combating the lethal nexus of drug trafficking and terrorism requires a bold and proactive approach. And as crime increasingly goes global, and national security threats remain global, the long arm of the law has to get even longer.[89]

Meanwhile, some observers have raised questions about the implementation of 21 U.S.C. 960a and related statutes in practice. Some have questioned whether the U.S. government approach to investigating and, ultimately, prosecuting individuals under 21 U.S.C. 960a sufficiently targets the most significant foreign drug and terrorism threats to U.S. interests.[90] Others question whether pursuit of foreign narco-terrorism suspects overseas and subsequent prosecution in U.S. courts is the most appropriate policy tool choice.

Looking Ahead: Implications for Congress

Policy issues related to the interaction of international crime and terrorism are inherently complex. While the U.S. government has maintained substantial long-standing efforts to combat terrorism and transnational crime separately, questions remain about how and whether issues related to the interaction of the two threats are handled most effectively across the multiple U.S. agencies involved. Efforts to combat transnational crime can result in positive and negative outcomes with counterterrorism policies, raising fundamental questions about how to prioritize combating crime or terrorism aspects of a case when both elements are present. Further, questions remain on how links between terrorist-criminal activity and potentially related U.S. polices—

---

[89] DOJ, "United States v. Henareh, et al., and Taza Gul Alizai," prepared remarks for U.S. Attorney Preet Bharara, July 26, 2011.

[90] See, for example, John E. Thomas, Jr. "Narco-Terrorism: Could the Legislative and Prosecutorial Responses Threaten Our Civil Liberties?" *Washington and Lee Law Review*, Vol. 66 (2009), pp. 1881-1920; Johnny Dwyer, "The DEA's Terrorist Hunters: Overreaching Their Authority?," *Time Magazine*, August 8, 2011; Benjamin Weiser, "For Prosecutors in New York, A Global Beat," *The News York Times*, March 28, 2011; Mike Scarcella, "Define Narco-Terrorist: The DEA's Expanded Enforcement Power Faces its First Appellate Case," *The National Law Journal*, November 21, 2011.

including but not limited to WMD proliferation, cyber security, post-conflict reconstruction efforts, and counterinsurgency—are integrated across agencies.

Since the September 11 attacks, Congress has enacted several landmark bills that have given the U.S. government greater authority and additional tools to counter the convergence of organized crime and terrorism. Less than six weeks after the attack, Congress enacted the USA PATRIOT Act (P.L. 107-56) to strengthen the U.S. government's ability to detect, report, and prevent terrorist activities, including potential connections between organized crime and terrorism.[91] Additionally, Congress enacted the Intelligence Reform and Terrorism Prevention Act of 2004 (P.L. 108-458) and the USA PATRIOT Improvement and Reauthorization Act of 2005 (P.L. 109-177), which further enhanced U.S. government efforts to crack down on terrorist financing and money laundering.[92]

Based on recent U.S. assessments, transnational crime and international terrorism appear to intersect and overlap in ways that will, at times, affect U.S. national interests. To this end, Congress may choose to continue to evaluate existing approaches and programs to combat the confluence of crime and terrorism through hearings and requesting or legislating reports to be issued by relevant executive branch agencies and inspector general offices. Congress may also choose to modify, adapt, or enhance existing legislative authorities and mandates to target various dimensions of the problem. Such approaches may be region- or group-specific, or global in scope.

More broadly, as policymakers consider the crime-terrorism nexus issue and relevant policy responses, key questions for Congress may include the following:

- What is the scope of the crime-terrorism issue? What types of crimes are involved? Which groups and actors of both kinds pose the greatest threat to U.S. national security?

- What political, social, economic, geographic, and demographic circumstances facilitate the interaction between transnational crime and international terrorism?

- Has the United States successfully exploited the partnering arrangements and differences in motivations and capabilities of terrorist groups and criminal organizations? If so, what lessons learned could apply to current and future activities by such actors?

- What prevents the U.S. government and international community from disrupting and dismantling current crime-terrorism threats?

---

[91] The PATRIOT Act, for example, stiffened money laundering penalties, granted the Secretary of the Treasury new powers, established mechanisms to report money laundering transactions through private banks, permitted the transfer of financial records among agencies if relevant to intelligence activities, created Federal jurisdiction over foreign money launderers, and made licensed money senders, including informal hawala networks, subject to mandatory reports on transactions.

[92] Among other provisions, the Intelligence Reform and Terrorism Prevention Act of 2004 expanded the authority and tools of the Department of the Treasury's Financial Crimes Enforcement Network (FinCEN), directed the Secretary of the Treasury to prescribe regulations requiring financial institutions to report certain cross-border money transfers, and directed the president to submit to Congress a report evaluating U.S. efforts to curtail international financing of terrorism. Pertaining to potential crime-terrorism connections, the USA PATRIOT Improvement and Reauthorization Act of 2005 increased penalties for terrorism financing, expanded the purview of the Racketeer Influenced and Corrupt Organizations (RICO) Act (P.L. 91-452), broadened the parameters of money laundering offenses, and made the receipt of military training from a foreign terrorist organization a predicate to a money laundering offense.

- Which federal government entities have the lead roles for addressing various aspects of the crime-terrorism phenomenon?

- How are government funds being spent to address concerns about crime-terrorism links?

- Is there a need to expand or adjust existing congressional authorities to combat the combined crime-terrorism threat? Are the available U.S. foreign policy tools sufficient to meet today's crime-terrorism concerns—and are such tools effectively implemented? If not, what can be improved?

Appendix. Terrorist Links to Criminal Financing

The following table summarizes the State Department's descriptions of how current foreign terrorist organizations (FTOs) raise funds and whether, if at all, an FTO is involved in criminal activities as a source of revenue. Among the 51 FTOs described in the State Department's most recent Country Reports on Terrorism (from May 2013), sources of funding vary. Common sources of funding include, in various combination, state sponsors, private donors, other terrorist groups, legitimate business activity, proceeds of crime. Popular forms criminal financing include extortion, kidnapping for ransom, drug trafficking, robbery, human smuggling, weapons smuggling, other contraband smuggling, money laundering, bank fraud, credit card fraud, cybercrime, immigration fraud, passport falsification, and illegal charcoal production. For 9 of the 51 FTOs, the State Department reports that funding sources and mechanisms are "unknown."

Table A-1. Foreign Terrorist Organization (FTOs): Reported Sources of External Aid

based on the State Department's *2012 Country Reports on Terrorism (2013)*

Foreign Terrorist Organization	Abbreviation	Designation Date	Criminal Financing?	Additional Description of Sources of Support
Revolutionary Organization 17 November	17N	October 8, 1997		Funding and external aid are "unknown."
Asbat al-Ansar	AAA	March 27, 2002		"It is likely that the group receives money through international Sunni extremist networks."
Abdallah Azzam Brigades	AAB	May 30, 2012		Funding and external aid are "unknown."
Al-Aqsa Martyrs Brigade	AAMB	March 27, 2002		"Iran has exploited AAMB's lack of resources and formal leadership by providing funds and guidance, mostly through Hizballah facilitators."
Ansar Al-Islam	AI	March 22, 2004		"AI receives assistance from a loose network of associates in Europe and the Middle East."
Al-Shabaab		March 18, 2008	Yes	"Al-Shabaab continued to have sufficient financing available.... " Sources include "funds from illegal charcoal production and exports from smaller ports along the coast, taxation of local populations and areas under al-Shabaab control, and foreign donations." It also receives "significant donations from the global Somali diaspora...."
Abu Nidal Organization	ANO	October 8, 1997		"The ANO's current access to resources is unclear, but it is likely that the decline in support previously provided by Libya, Syria, and Iran has had a severe impact on its capabilities."
Army of Islam	AOI	May 19, 2011	Yes	"AOI receives the bulk of its funding from a variety of criminal activities in Gaza."

Foreign Terrorist Organization	Abbreviation	Designation Date	Criminal Financing?	Additional Description of Sources of Support
Al-Qa'ida	AQ	October 8, 1999		"AQ primarily depends on donations from like-minded supporters as well as from individuals who believe that their money is supporting a humanitarian cause. Some funds are diverted from Islamic charitable organizations." Additionally, as previous opportunities "for receiving and sending funds have become more difficult to access, several affiliates have engaged in kidnapping for ransom. Through kidnapping for ransom operations and other criminal activities, the affiliates have also increased their financial independence." AQ and Hizballah sympathizers located in South America and the Caribbean "continued to provide financial and ideological support ...."
Al-Qa'ida in the Arabian Peninsula	AQAP	January 10, 2010	Yes	"AQAP's funding primarily comes from robberies and kidnap for ransom operations and to a lesser degree from donations from like-minded supporters."
Al-Qa'ida in Iraq	AQI	December 17, 2004 (amended December 11, 2011)	Yes	"AQI receives most of its funding from a variety of businesses and criminal activities within Iraq."
Al-Qa'ida in the Islamic Maghreb (formerly the Salafist Group for Call and Combat)	AQIM (formerly GSPC)	March 27, 2002 (amended February 20, 2008)	Yes	"AQIM members engaged in kidnapping for ransom and criminal activities to finance their operations." Kidnapping operations, which typically targeted those with an "established pattern of making concessions in the form of ransom payments ... ", reportedly "continued to yield significant sums for AQIM.... " Additionally, "Algerian expatriates and AQIM supporters abroad – many residing in Western Europe – may also provide limited financial and logistical support."
Abu Sayyaf Group	ASG	October 8, 1997	Yes	"The ASG is funded through kidnapping for ransom operations and extortion, and many also receive funding from external sources such as remittances from overseas Philippines workers and Middle East-based violent extremists. In the past, the ASG has also received assistance from regional terrorist groups such as Jemaah Islamiya, whose operatives provided training to ASG members and helped facilitate several ASG terrorist attacks."
United Self-Defense Forces of Colombia	AUC	September 10, 2001	Yes	"As much as 70 percent of the AUC's paramilitary operations costs were financed with drug-related earnings. Some former members of the AUC never demobilized or are recidivists, and these elements have continued to engage heavily in criminal activities."
Aum Shinrikyo	AUM	October 8, 1997		"Funding primarily comes from member contributions."
Continuity Irish Republican Army	CIRA	July 13, 2004	Yes	"CIRA supported its activities through criminal activities, including smuggling." The group carries out "bombings, assassinations, kidnappings, hijackings, extortion, and robberies."
Communist Party of the Philippines / New People's Army	CPP/NPP	August 9, 2002	Yes	"The CPP/NPA raises funds through extortion."

Foreign Terrorist Organization	Abbreviation	Designation Date	Criminal Financing?	Additional Description of Sources of Support
Revolutionary People's Liberation Party/Front	DHKP/C	October 8, 1997	Yes	"The DHKP/C finances its activities chiefly through donations and extortion and raises funds primarily in Europe."
Revolutionary Struggle	EA	May 18, 2009		Funding and external aid are "unknown."
National Liberation Army	ELN	October 8, 1997	Yes	"The ELN draws its funding from the narcotics trade and from extortion of oil and gas companies. Additional funds are derived from kidnapping ransoms. There is no known external aid."
Basque Fatherland and Liberty	ETA	October 8, 1997		"ETA is probably experiencing financial shortages given that the group announced publicly in September 2011 that it had ceased collecting 'revolutionary taxes' from Basque businesses. This extortion program was a major source of ETA's income."
Revolutionary Armed Forces of Colombia	FARC	October 8, 1997	Yes	"Today, it only nominally fights in support of Marxist goals, and is heavily involved in narcotics production and trafficking.... The FARC has well-documented ties to the full range of narcotics trafficking activities, including extortion, cultivation, and distribution." Some human smuggling in the Darien Region of Panama was "facilitated by FARC elements operating on both sides of the border."
Moroccan Islamic Combatant Group	GICM	October 11, 2005	Yes	"In the past, GICM has been involved in narcotics trafficking in North Africa and Europe to fund its operations."
Hamas		October 8, 1997	Yes	"Hamas receives funding, weapons, and training from Iran. In addition, the group raises funds in the Persian Gulf countries and receives donations from Palestinian expatriates around the world, through its charities, such as the umbrella fundraising organization, the Union of Good. Some fundraising and propaganda activity also takes place in Western Europe." Hamas, among others, "smuggled weapons, cash, and other contraband into Gaza through an extensive network of tunnels from Egypt." The group is also known to "retain a cadre of leaders and facilitators that conduct political, fundraising, and arms-smuggling activities throughout the region."
Hizballah		October 8, 1997	Yes	"Iran continues to provide Hizballah with training, weapons, and explosives, as well as political, diplomatic, monetary, and organizational aid; Syria furnished training, weapons, diplomatic, and political support. Hizballah also receives funding from private donations and profits from legal and illegal businesses. Hizballah receives financial support from Lebanese Shia communities in Europe, Africa, South America, North America, and Asia. As illustrated by the Lebanese Canadian bank case, Hizballah supporters are often engaged in a range of criminal activities that benefit the group financially. These have included smuggling contraband goods, passport falsification, trafficking in narcotics, money laundering, and credit card, immigration, and bank fraud." AQ and Hizballah sympathizers located South American and Caribbean "continued to provide financial and ideological support.... "

Foreign Terrorist Organization	Abbreviation	Designation Date	Criminal Financing?	Additional Description of Sources of Support
Haqqani Network	HQN	September 19, 2012	Yes	HQN draws strength through cooperation with other terrorist organizations operating in Afghanistan, including the Afghan Taliban, al-Qa'ida, Tehrik-e Taliban Pakistan, the Islamic Movement of Uzbekistan, Lashkar-e Jhangvi, and Jaish-e Mohammad." In addition to such cooperative support, "HQN receives much of its funds from donors in Pakistan and the Gulf, as well as through criminal activities such as kidnappings, extortion, smuggling, and other licit and illicit business ventures."
Harakat-ul Jihad Islami	HUJI	August 6, 2010		Funding and external aid are "unknown."
Harakat ul-Jihad-i-Islami/Bangladesh	HUJI-B	March 5, 2008		"HUJI-B funding comes from a variety of sources. Several international Muslim NGOs may have funneled money to HUJI-B and other Bangladeshi militant groups."
Harakat ul-Hujahideen	HUM	October 8, 1997		"HUM collects donations from wealthy and grassroots donors in Pakistan. HUM's financial collection methods include soliciting donations in magazine advertisements and pamphlets."
Gama'a Al-Islamiyya	IG	October 8, 1997		Funding and external aid are "unknown."
Islamic Jihad Union	IJU	June 17, 2005		Funding and external aid are "unknown."
Islamic Movement of Uzbekistan	IMU	September 20, 2000		"The IMU receives support from a large Uzbek diaspora, terrorist organizations, and donors from Europe, Central and South Asia, and the Middle East."
Indian Mujahedeen	IM	September 19, 2011		"Suspected to obtain funding and support from other terrorist organizations, such as LeT and HUJI, and from sources in Pakistan and the Middle East."
Jemaah Ansharut Tauhid	JAT	March 13, 2012	Yes	"JAT raises funds through membership donations, as well as bank robberies, cyber hacking, and other illicit activities; and legitimate business activities such as operating bookstores and other shops." Bank robberies and other illicit activities are carried out "to fund the purchase of assault weapons, ammunition, explosives, and bomb-making materials."
Jaish-e-Mohammed	JEM	December 26, 2001		JEM "collects funds through donation requests in magazines and pamphlets, sometimes using charitable causes to solicit donations." Since 2007, "JEM has withdrawn funds from bank accounts and invested in legal businesses, such as commodity trading, real estate, and production of consumer goods."
Jemaah Islamiya	JI	October 23, 2002	Yes	"Investigations have indicated that JI is fully capable of its own fundraising through membership donations and criminal and business activities. It has received financial, ideological, and logistical support from Middle Eastern contacts and NGOs."
Jundallah		November 4, 2010		Funding and external aid are "unknown."
Kahane Chai		October 8, 1997		"Receives support from sympathizers in the United States and Europe."
Kata'ib Hizballah	KH	July 2, 2009		"KH is almost entirely dependent on support from Iran and Lebanese Hizballah."

Foreign Terrorist Organization	Abbreviation	Designation Date	Criminal Financing?	Additional Description of Sources of Support
Lashkar e-Tayyiba	LeT	December 26, 2001		"LeT collects donations in Pakistan and the Gulf as well as from other donors in the Middle East and Europe, particularly the UK."
Libyan Islamic Fighting Group	LIFG	December 17, 2004		Funding and external aid are "unknown."
Lashkar I Jhangvi	LJ	January 30, 2003	Yes	"Funding comes from wealthy donors in Pakistan, as well as the Middle East, particularly Saudi Arabia. The group engages in criminal activity to fund its activities, including extortion and protection money."
Liberation Tigers of Tamil Eelam	LTTE	October 8, 1997	Yes	"The LTTE used its international contacts and the large Tamil diaspora in North America, Europe, and Asia to procure weapons, communications, funding, and other needed supplies. The group employed charities as fronts to collect and divert funds for their activities." The group's "financial network of support continued to operate throughout 2012, and there were multiple reports of increased LTTE involvement in human smuggling out of refugee camps."
Popular Front for the Liberation of Palestine	PFLP	October 8, 1997		"Leadership received safe haven in Syria."
Popular Front for the Liberation of Palestine-General Command	PFLP-GC	October 8, 1997		"The group's primary recent focus was supporting Hizballah's attacks against Israel, training members of other Palestinian terrorist groups, and smuggling weapons." PFLP-GC received "safe haven and logistical and military support from Syria and financial support from Iran."
Palestine Islamic Jihad—Shaqaqi Faction	PIJ	October 8, 1997		"Receives financial assistance and training primarily from Iran."
Kurdistan Workers' Party	PKK	October 8, 1997	Yes	"The PKK receives financial support from the large Kurdish diaspora in Europe and from criminal activity."
Palestine Liberation Front—Abu Abbas Faction	PLF	October 8, 1997		Funding and external aid are "unknown."
Real IRA	RIRA	May 16, 2001		"The RIRA is suspected of receiving funds from sympathizers in the United States and of attempting to buy weapons from U.S. gun dealers. The RIRA was also reported to have purchased sophisticated weapons from the Balkans and to have occasionally collaborated with the Continuity Irish Republican Army."
Shining Path	SL	October 8, 1997	Yes	"SL is primarily funded by the narcotics trade."
Tehrik-e Taliban Pakistan	TTP	September 1, 2010	Yes	"TTP is believed to raise most of its funds through kidnapping for ransom and operations that target Afghanistan-bound military transport trucks for robbery. Such operations allow TTP to steal military equipment, which it sells in Afghan and Pakistani markets."

Source: U.S. Department of State, *Country Reports on Terrorism 2012*, May 2013.

Author Contact Information

John Rollins
Specialist in Terrorism and National Security
jrollins@crs.loc.gov, 7-5529

Liana Sun Wyler
Analyst in International Crime and Narcotics
lwyler@crs.loc.gov, 7-6177

Acknowledgments

Updates to this report continue to benefit from the substantive contributions provided by Seth Rosen, former research associate at CRS in 2009.